GOING LIVE

GOING LIVE

Getting the News Right in a Real-Time, Online World

PHILIP SEIB

ROWMAN & LITTLEFIELD PUBLISHERS, INC.
Lanham • Boulder • New York • Oxford

ROWMAN & LITTLEFIELD PUBLISHERS, INC.

Published in the United States of America
by Rowman & Littlefield Publishers, Inc.
4720 Boston Way, Lanham, Maryland 20706
http://www.rowmanlittlefield.com

12 Hid's Copse Road, Cumnor Hill, Oxford OX2 9JJ, England

British Library Cataloguing in Publication Information Available

Library of Congress Cataloging-in-Publication Data
Seib, Philip M., 1949–
    Going live : getting the news right in a real-time, online world / Philip
Seib.
    p. cm.
    Includes bibliographical references and index.
    ISBN 0-7425-0900-1 (alk. paper)
    1. Television broadcasting of news. 2. Live television programs.
3. Radio journalism. 4. Electronic journals. I. Title.
    PN4784.T4 S45   2001
    070.1'95—dc21   00-042562

Printed in the United States of America

⊗ ™ The paper used in this publication meets the minimum requirements of
American National Standard for Information Sciences—Permanence of Paper
for Printed Library Materials, ANSI/NISO Z39.48-1992.

For Charles and Shirley Seib

CONTENTS

PREFACE

This is a book about continuity and change. The twentieth century was the era of radio and then television, which revolutionized the way society functions by informing, educating, entertaining, and sometimes outraging or inflaming. As conveyors of news, radio and television cultivated a mass audience and held a competitive advantage over print media because of the timeliness and vividness of their coverage. Radio and television were not limited to reporting what had already happened; they could present the event itself *as* it happened. As years passed, increasingly sophisticated technology made this kind of reporting easier and more common. Going live became the trademark for broadcast and then cable news.

Audiences presumably are more attentive to live coverage because they are caught up in the suspenseful uncertainty of the moment. They do not merely learn about the story, they experience it—seeing it unfold and being tugged by the ebb and flow of events.

Going live is exciting and dramatic. But is it good journalism? With live coverage now feasible from virtually anywhere at any time, drama and excitement may overwhelm news judgment. Taste and common sense may be pushed aside in the rush to get on the air fast. The scrupulous allegiance to accuracy that should be the cornerstone of journalism is sometimes ignored because "there just isn't time" to check facts.

Cable and satellite carriers have fostered a proliferation of television offerings, and the pace of daily life—including the interminable "drive time"—has reinforced radio's popularity. But journalistic standards have not always kept up with technological advances. As the continuum of electronic news stretches into the future, significant doubts exist about the quality of the news product. There are two basic questions: Is radio and television news as good as it should be? If not, what can be done to make it better?

Emphasis on real-time news complicates the answers to such questions because speed and quality are not always compatible. "Real-time" means news as it is happening—live coverage (sometimes incorporating material taped shortly before). A journalist reporting an event as it occurs may feel compelled to ignore fundamental duties, such as securing corroboration and providing context. Those tasks take time, and the pressure to go live may keep the reporter tied to the microphone and camera instead of finding that one more source or confirming that extra bit of crucial information.

Time is a valuable tool in news gathering, and to give it up is risky. Print journalists have criticized their electronic colleagues for the sloppiness and superficiality that can characterize live reporting. Of course, newspapers and magazines have deadlines that put time pressure on their journalists, and wire services have long prided themselves on the speed with which they can report a story. But these are mostly intramural matters; a story completed just at deadline or a wire service report about a breaking event reaches the public only indirectly, passing first through an editorial process, even if a frantic one.

Now that is changing. Even print news organizations are

delivering their product electronically as well as on paper. The World Wide Web is the next major news medium. On the Web, newspapers and magazines can go live. By doing so, they compete more effectively with radio and television, but they give up the time that was a friend to judgment. They also find that part of their traditional culture has become obsolete. The system of the print newsroom was built upon a regular publishing schedule. For journalists crafting stories, the news cycle—daily for newspapers, longer for magazines—was as reliable as a metronome. No more. Morning newspapers such as the *Washington Post* are producing online editions at other times in the day and delivering updated reports at a moment's notice. The public has little tolerance for any sluggishness in regard to Web news.

Television and radio are also adapting to the realities of the Internet, creating their own Web sites as the online audience grows. For electronic news organizations, the Web allows expansion of real-time offerings. Networks and stations use their Web sites to offer "Netcasts"—initially supplements to regular news programming (such as expanded reporting of election night vote tallies), with unique content soon to follow. The sites also feature new and archived video and audio on demand.

Despite the nearly infinite capacity of the Internet, the online world is already getting crowded. The Web world of news is cluttered with sites that are delivering similar products. Only the most resolute Web junkies will partake of all this, and the new medium's economics are proving harsh for those whose sites do not have a well-known brand name or other appealing features. Many Web offerings will disappear as others merge with former competitors. On the Web, the products of the *New York Times* and ABC News will be very much alike in their mix of text, audio, and video. The logical next step is the joint enterprise. This is convergence—news organizations from different media coming together in the new medium. Added to this mix are entities, such as MSNBC, that are created to exist partly or entirely on the Web.

This book examines where real-time news coverage has been, where it is today, and where it is going. Emphasis is placed not just on the ability to go live but on the quality of the real-time news product. "Journalism ethics" is not an oxymoron; there are few professions in which ethical issues get more day-to-day attention than they receive in the news business. Real-time reporting enhances the already substantial power of the news media, which makes essential the good faith and good judgment of those who provide that coverage. This is the key to ethical journalism, but it requires more than instinct. The issues of real-time news demand thoughtful consideration that can serve as the foundation for making real-time ethical decisions.

The antecedents of today's Web news are found in live radio and television reports, some of which have historical import of their own: Edward R. Murrow's broadcasts during the blitz of London, the coverage of John F. Kennedy's assassination and funeral, reports from the bombing of Baghdad and the missile attacks of the Gulf War.

Less momentous but more common are the live stories that punctuate national and local newscasts. Sometimes these stories are important, but too often they are pointless or tasteless, hyped relentlessly in efforts to transform the mundane into the consequential. Going live can become an addiction that overwhelms news standards, such as television coverage of suicides as they happen. Some consultants urge local news directors to adopt "live, local, and late-breaking" as the formula for garnering higher ratings. If an event has ended several hours before the newscast airs, no matter; put a reporter on the scene for a live report anyway. It may be silly, but it's live.

The advent of the Internet is just the latest reshaping of the

TV news business. During television's early years, the big networks dominated to the point that most viewers watched them or watched nothing. Cable (and later satellite) television changed all that, making dozens, then hundreds of channels available. This gave the public lots of choices about what to watch, but it meant that the revenue pie, which did not expand as rapidly, had to be cut into narrower and narrower slices. As viewers dispersed among the new channels, so too did advertisers' dollars.

This has produced not just economic realignments but also shifts in coverage content. In 2000, the broadcast networks ceded a considerable portion of their political coverage prerogatives to cable. Part of this was a function of the ownership and management of news organizations by non-news corporations and executives. Making money sometimes conflicts with serving the public. Given this business context, the television news Web product will merit careful scrutiny as it develops.

Print news organizations, which have long had to compete with electronic media, now face unsettling challenges from Web offerings. These are not just journalistic matters but also include the possibility that online competitors will undermine newspapers' economic foundation. Classified ads, which provide 30 percent of newspaper income, are well suited for the Web. Newspapers simply cannot allow that revenue to be taken away from them, so they must respond with online products of their own. To a considerable extent, the caliber of newspapers' online news product will depend on how well they can master online economics.

While this evolutionary struggle proceeds, newspaper newsrooms are reshaping themselves to produce on-paper and online journalism. Much of this process involves trial-and-error innovation, and the errors are getting lots of attention. Coverage of the White House sex scandal in 1998 and 1999 showed that newspapers, like their electronic counterparts, can find the real-time world a treacherous place.

In the background loom difficult questions. Who is the new media journalist? Is he or she a traditional reporter with a few new skills, or a technical whiz with a smattering of knowledge about journalism? Should the Web site be allowed to scoop the parent news organization, or will that pull readers away from what is still the principal moneymaker? Wrestling with such issues, along with logistical matters, can push ethical concerns into the background.

News organizations must improve and compete; that's nothing new. But now they must also contemplate convergence, which adds a dimension to their journalistic and economic prospects. Even in their infancy, online competitors are ferocious. The number of Americans using the Web is multiplying explosively, so trying to eradicate the online competition is not an option. Virtually every "old media" news organization has no choice but to develop an online presence. The biggest question is not whether an established news organization will develop a Web identity but whether it will abandon its previous, pre-Internet incarnation entirely. Will the newspaper cease to exist except electronically? Is the television era over?

Such issues create a tumultuous environment in which to do journalism. As news organizations adjust to new economics and new technology, new dimensions of ethics must develop. The online world is a real-time world, so the next refinement of journalism ethics should place special emphasis on the responsibilities that accompany the delivery of news as it is happening.

Journalism's credibility depends largely on the public's belief that the women and men who deliver the news operate in good faith, trying to present information fairly and accurately. The news media's record is far from unblemished, but most journalists genuinely want to do a good, and then a better, job. Perhaps this book will help.

ACKNOWLEDGMENTS

Many people helped create this book. Brenda Hadenfeldt at Rowman & Littlefield was a believer in this project from the beginning. Others who supplied ideas and encouragement include Bill Elliott, Marty Haag, Dick Mason, and Bob Mong. And Christine Wicker provided the faith and love that make everything possible.

GOING LIVE

1

THE WORLD IS WATCHING

Scene 1: The man with the rifle has been holding police at bay for several hours on the Los Angeles freeway. He has fired some shots but hasn't hit anyone.

Local television stations are providing live, nonstop coverage of the standoff from their helicopters and ground units. Two of the stations have broken into after-school children's programming to do so.

Finally, the man places his weapon under his chin. The television stations do not break away or pull back from their tight shots. A few seconds later, the man pulls the trigger. He dies at the scene.

In their living rooms, viewers see it all. This is state-of-the-art journalism. It's fast, it's fascinating, it's live.

Scene 2: The reporter calls the White House press office in midafternoon with a sensational story. He seeks confirmation of his information that a White House steward has told a federal grand jury that he witnessed President Clinton and Monica Lewinsky alone together in the president's study. The White House spokesman, knowing that the reporter's newspaper is a morning publication, says he will check on the report and respond promptly.

Moments later, the reporter tells the spokesman that the story has just been posted on the paper's Web site. Shortly after that, the paper's Washington bureau chief is discussing it on a cable news channel. Ninety minutes—an eternity—later, the steward's lawyer issues a statement saying the paper's story is incorrect.

1

As it turns out, the paper had a crucial fact wrong. But, fearing that competitors were on the trail of the same story, editors decided not to wait for the White House response before publishing online. Being the first, being the fastest, was more important.

T hese two cases, discussed in more detail later in the book, reflect a pronounced trend in the news business: increased emphasis on speed of delivery of the news product, sometimes at the cost of traditional journalistic standards.

No one will disagree that timeliness is an important ingredient of the news. There is, however, plenty of debate about just *how* important it should be. Should emphasis on speed of delivery override judgments about relevance and taste? Should it supersede the commitment to accuracy? Is the audience so hungry for immediate news that traditional editorial processes should be set aside in favor of a technology-driven system that presents events as they happen?

These questions are not new, but they have become harder to answer as real-time coverage has moved from being exceptional to being standard in the news business. This evolution has proceeded steadily as news delivery mechanisms have expanded from radio to broadcast television to cable to the Internet. A continuum exists, linking these media that, although they are different in many ways, share the ability to deliver real-time news.

It is hard to identify any single dominant turning point in the journey from delayed to instantaneous news, although the relatively recent arrival of the Cable News Network certainly changed expectations and attitudes among news consumers and news professionals. Even more significant than breaking a brand-new story (which doesn't happen that often) is the steady updating of developing news. CNN and other all-news providers offer reiterated and sometimes refreshed versions of a story. They are always ready with an answer to the question, What's new? Human curiosity being what it is, that approach has innate appeal, and other news organizations—print as well as electronic—have been working on ways to satisfy that curiosity.

With computers in the offices and homes of a rapidly growing number of Americans, the World Wide Web has become the latest journalistic phenomenon. A click on any of the many Internet news sites brings the latest bulletin to the screen, in text, and, increasingly, in audio and video forms as well. How great a transformation of the news business this new medium will bring about has not yet been precisely determined, but it will certainly be profound. A preliminary look at the impact of the Internet helps put the entire evolution of real-time news in context.

THE RISE OF THE INTERNET

Despite its impact on so many aspects of modern life, television coverage, as we know it, may soon be superseded by new forms of news delivery. The number of Internet users is growing rapidly; by some accounts in 1998 it was doubling every hundred days. By September 1998, the number of users in the United States was reported to have reached 70 million, roughly a quarter of the American population. A study released in February 2000 concluded that 55 percent of Americans had access to the Internet.

A survey conducted in late 1998 for the Pew Research Center for the People and the Press found that the percentage of Americans getting news from the Internet at least once a week had risen from 4 percent in 1995 to 26 percent in December 1998. Of those who go online to get news, only 11 percent reported that they were using other news sources less often than before.[1] Another Pew survey, conducted a year later, found that 30 percent of the public was going online for news.[2]

As the Internet use base grows to include more casual news

Table 1.1   Network News Viewership

Percent Who Watch	1993	1995	1996	1998
Regularly	60	48	42	38
Sometimes	28	28	29	28
Hardly ever	5	14	15	15
Never	6	10	14	19

Source: Pew Research Center for the People and the Press.

consumers (as well as "news junkies"), Internet use might more often replace, rather than supplement, other news sources. Perhaps foreshadowing this shift is the pronounced downward trend in nightly network news viewership (see table 1.1).[3] Beyond the nightly newscasts, the networks' magazine and morning shows have substantial audiences. The magazine shows, which proliferated during the late 1990s, have expanded their base, particularly among younger viewers.[4]

One theory about these findings is that the headline service provided by nightly newscasts is more easily duplicated by the Internet, whereas the feature-oriented chat of the morning shows and the minidocumentary style of the magazine programs remain—so far—outside the repertoire of most Internet news providers. Another element is the popularity of cable news networks. The Pew survey found that 40 percent of Americans report that they regularly watch CNN, CNBC, MSNBC, or the Fox News Channel (60 percent when ESPN and Weather Channel viewers are added). The principal reason cited for the popularity of cable news is its reliable immediacy.[5] At CNN, for example, network officials don't have to worry about bumping a popular soap opera if a big story breaks in the middle of the day. Viewers know that they will always find news on the news channels. The news audience grows considerably larger when a major story is breaking, times when cable networks attract their largest viewership.

An example of this kind of story was the stock market nose-dive on October 27, 1997. A Pew Center study found that "all-news cable television was the top source for highly attentive news consumers tracking the story," attracting 35 percent of this audience. Note that these viewers are part of a special subset of the overall audience—"highly attentive" and "tracking" this particular story.

Perhaps a more interesting aspect of the audience for this story was the use of the Internet by news consumers. Just 3 percent of the "attentive audience" first learned of the market drop via the Internet, but 11 percent followed the story online during the day. According to the Pew study, nearly half of the primary audience for this story who had online capability followed the stock market on the Internet that day.[6] To a certain extent, this example is a function of the nature of the 1997 Internet audience—a group skewed upward in education and income, likely to be especially interested in a big stock market story. Also, many of these people probably were at work, with easier access to a computer than to a television. As the Internet user base broadens, breaking news stories about more diverse topics will attract more of this online tracking.

An important factor spurring more Internet use and fostering this expansion of the audience is the declining cost of home computers. Between January 1996 and January 1998, the average selling price for home personal computers dropped from about $1,700 to less than $1,200, with an increasing number available for less than $1,000. By mid-2000, decent personal computers could be purchased for less than $500. A Forrester Research study reports that the 43 percent of U.S. households with personal computers in 1998 is expected to climb to 60 percent by 2002. The study also found an important effect of the decline in PC prices: more than 70 percent of new PC buyers will have incomes under $50,000.[7]

Clearly, shifts are taking place in the ways Americans get

their news. Between 1960 and 1995, daily newspaper circulation held at approximately 60 million while the country's population grew from 180 million to 260 million. Thus per capita readership dropped by about a third, a trend that may accelerate because newspaper readership is twice as weak among those under thirty as among those over sixty-five.[8] According to the Newspaper Association of America, daily circulation had fallen to around 56 million in 1998.

During much of that time, television was the principal beneficiary of the newspapers' loss in readers. But today, television also is vulnerable. Andy Grove, president and CEO of Intel Corporation, has predicted that home computer use—much of it online—will exceed television viewing by the year 2000. Grove said that by mid-1996, more than 18 million people were spending five hours a week on the Internet.[9] By early 2000, television had not succumbed as Grove had predicted, but a Stanford University study reported that 36 percent of Americans with Internet access were spending at least five hours online each week.[10]

The number of people and the number of hours continue to grow, and some of that time was once spent watching television. Advertisers certainly take note of this, particularly because many of those who are watching their computers instead of their televisions are the more affluent people many marketers target.

As the new computer-based media evolve and their audiences grow, the word being heard more and more is "convergence." In journalism, that means a growing similarity in news presentation through various media. In technology, it means a search for a common site where the products of these various media will be delivered. Competition between television screen and computer screen for the consumer's attention may prove economically impractical because there are unlikely to be enough advertising dollars to sustain both television and computer-based media. That means increasing use of one screen for both—the Web TV concept.

Convergence involves marrying the slick format of television to the almost infinite information-providing capacity of the Internet. The potential offspring of this marriage could be enormously appealing:

- Watching news and entertainment programming with an array of links to related material. Want to compare a president's speech to one by a predecessor? Pull up the text and/or the video of the earlier talk; put them on split screen if you like. If the president refers to an incident from Cold War days, pull up an index on your screen and find a text or documentary to check later. Watching the latest sitcom and yearn for an early *Seinfeld* instead? Just tell your computer and Jerry will appear. (Whether—or more likely how—a fee will be charged for this is yet to be determined.)
- Watching what you like when you like. Television's traditional channels and schedules will be meaningless. You'll be able to create your own channel containing only the programs you want, and they will be stored on a microchip so you'll be able to watch them whenever you want. And—to the dismay of advertisers—you'll be able to eliminate the commercials.
- Having quick, simple access to information for your exclusive use. Planning a trip to London next month? Check the British newspapers and television networks to see what's going on. Compare airfares and hotel rates and then make reservations; check the weather forecast; get theater reviews and buy tickets; look at a travel channel program about tourist sites and then design a walking tour and print your map. Organizing the whole trip can be done thoroughly and easily.

Whether the consumer is getting hard news, watching a sitcom, planning a trip, or doing all these, reliance on the television-computer combination will be useful and possibly addictive. Add games, shopping, and other Web surfing attractions to the mix, and it becomes clear just how vigorously news organizations will have to compete for the audience's attention.

For news organizations, this competition could prove distracting. Just as broadcast news professionals have had to balance the demands of good journalism with those of good television, so too will Internet journalists be juggling their basic professional responsibilities with the need to devise an appealing new media product. With the individual news consumer having greater choice about what information he or she wants, journalists' role in judging what news the public *needs* may change. Today it is possible to engage in a certain amount of force-feeding. If ABC News, for example, decides that its audience should be aware of the latest crisis in the Balkans, it can put stories about it on the air and presumably at least part of the audience will take notice. If, however, in the new media era, visitors to ABC's Web site consistently ignore the international news offerings on the site's menu of stories, news executives may be tempted to cut back their overseas coverage.

Among other important decisions about how much and what kind of news to provide will be those involving links, which are the electronic connections between Web sites. Links provide access to the supplemental information that can make Internet news dissemination so useful. A story about Social Security reform that appears on a news organization's site could feature links to the sites of sources used in the story, such as members of Congress, the Social Security Administration, the American Association of Retired Persons, a university think tank, and so on. Underlying this is an important issue: If a news organization features a link to a source's site, are journalists vouching for the accuracy of the information at that site? News consumers could reasonably assume that by offering the link the news organization implicitly puts a journalistic stamp of approval on the secondary site. Or does it? Writing in the *Media Studies Journal*, the Associated Press's Elizabeth Weise offered the example of a controversial 1996 series in the *San Jose Mercury News* about possible ties between the CIA and cocaine dealing in Los Angeles: "Whether or not you believe the premise of the story, the paper's Web site made masterful use of the new medium by linking every source and reference it had to the online version—letting the reader, not the reporter decide on the credibility of the claims."[11]

This may become the standard procedure, fostering an intellectual open market for news consumers to pick and choose among varied offerings, based on the assumption that these news consumers will discriminate wisely in their evaluations and choices. "Let the buyer [reader] beware" would be the controlling principle in terms of policing content. That approach certainly is the most expedient, but it also could be considered ethical buck passing. To complicate the issue further, suppose the source's site has its own links to still more sites. Even if the news organization takes some responsibility for the links it offers, how far along the chain does that responsibility extend?

News organizations' Web sites will compete not only among themselves but also with nonjournalistic providers of similar information. Politicians, for instance, will make good use of the Web, using it to circumvent the news media when delivering their messages to voters. Candidates' Web sites will provide the latest news and information from the campaign in the way they want it to reach voters. The filter of journalism will be removed. These sites will also be designed to meet the interests of individual voters, providing a menu of issues from which the site's visitors can select just those that appeal to them.

This is a profound shift in the balance of power between politicians and journalists. Candidates and voters alike have assumed that reporters will scrutinize political messages, analyze their content, and then deliver some while ignoring others. Candidates can partly evade this through advertising, but no candidate can afford to buy anywhere near the amount of advertising that would match the flow of news.

The Internet is the great equalizer. Any politician can create a Web site at low cost that is unfettered by picky journalists. The Web can be used to solicit contributions and recruit volunteers, both of which John McCain did with great success during the 2000 presidential campaign. (His campaign raised $810,000 online within forty-eight hours of his upset victory in the New Hampshire primary.) With its ever improving video and audio capabilities, the Web can take campaign events into voters' homes. Moving beyond the site itself, e-mail can reach millions of voters and allow two-way communication between politician and public. Anyone who registered on Al Gore's e-mail list during the 2000 campaign would never be lonely, receiving campaign messages almost daily.

All this cyberpoliticking sounds wonderful, a valuable enhancement of democracy. But it also raises important questions, especially about a redefined role for journalists. Much of the politician-generated Internet product is information that looks like "news" but has not undergone journalistic scrutiny. When the press is removed from its role as interlocutor, a barrier to propaganda and untruth is eliminated.

Some news consumers might not mind that. They're happy to wade through the deluge of information and make their own judgments, unimpeded by the bias that they believe infects the press. Many other people, however, rely on journalists to evaluate the material politicians churn out and add different views. They want the press to separate news from nonsense.

News organizations need to adjust to politicians' rapidly expanding use of the Internet. They should start covering candidates' Web sites and introduce truth testing of Web content, such as has proved helpful in policing campaign ads.

Beyond paying attention to politicians' sites, news organizations can use the Internet to expand their own coverage. The Internet can provide a home for massive amounts of information: issues analysis, voting records, candidates' biographies, speech excerpts, lists of contributors, polling data, and other raw stuff of politics. News sites can also offer links to partisan and nonpartisan sites.

For political junkies, the Web can be heaven. And for interested, if not fanatical, political observers, news Web sites can provide basics such as comparisons of candidates' voting records and locations of polling places.

By the time the 2004 presidential campaign begins, most Americans will be using the Internet daily, and online campaigning will be standard. Politicians will send voters personalized e-mail about their favorite issues. Fund-raising appeals will flow steadily through the Web, as will get-out-the-vote exhortations on election day. Candidates will compete to offer the most attractive sites, with ever fancier graphics and audio and video content. News organizations will also battle for attention with their own flashy sites.

As reliance on the Web increases, news organizations should not succumb to gimmickry or to focusing exclusively on news for political insiders. They should not forget the importance of offering easy access to information for casually interested voters. These are the people whose participation is always in doubt and who need to be pulled closer to the heart of politics. Perhaps knowing more will spur them to do more. News organizations should also take full advantage of the Web's interactive features, encouraging news consumers to critique not only the politicians but also the political coverage.

This will require lots of work, but if journalists fail to use the Web in these ways they will be left behind by the politicians and the public, becoming the dinosaurs of the new, Internet-driven political era.

Structuring the news inventory will require care. To keep their audience, news organizations will have to allow news consumers to pick and choose, and "force-feeding" information about issues that journalists judge to be important might not work. Presumably, the news sites will provide links to the politicians' sites. This could lead back to those questions about responsibility for links. Suppose a candidate's site includes an inaccurate, damaging attack on an opponent. Will the voter who has reached that site via a link from a news organization's site be more inclined to assume that the charges are accurate?

On election day, the Web will be the political junkies' paradise. Voting returns and projections can be fed to the audience constantly, with site visitors picking the races that they want to watch. No more waiting while television journalists work their way through a lengthy list of contests in which the particular viewer has no interest. Again, the Web site is ideal for meeting individualized interests. In 1996, the audience demand for election night information was so great that it overwhelmed some major news organizations' sites. MSNBC's site had to shut down for an hour soon after East Coast voting ended because it was overwhelmed by the number of visitors. That kind of problem will certainly be resolved as Web technology improves.

In the young life of the Internet, a milestone was reached in September 1998, when independent counsel Kenneth Starr released his report alleging that President Clinton had committed impeachable offenses. People around the world could get their first look at the report by going online to read it. Journalists offered summaries of the report's contents, and news organizations' Web sites provided links to the document. But, in many ways, the news media were merely bystanders while readers who wanted to wade into the report's allegations did so on their own.

Government documents had been electronically accessible for some time, but never before had the Internet been so widely promoted and widely used as a source for information about a breaking news story. CBS, for example, reported that on the day the Starr report was released, the network's Web site was receiving up to 10,000 requests per second for the material.

The Starr report example is significant on several levels. On one, the electronic openness is a facet of information age democracy. Government is increasingly accessible to anyone using the Internet. On the other hand, it marks a change in the relationship between the news media and the public, with the Internet as information provider displacing news organizations.

Another case from September 1998 underscores this change. After the crash of Swissair flight 111, in which all 229 on board died, the airline used its Web site to disseminate information about the accident and its aftermath. Anyone going to that site found a long list of Swissair news releases, all available at the click of a home computer's mouse.

After being posted on their sources' Web sites, releases may be picked up by news services and disseminated through their sites. When the release is about a business—especially a prediction about a change in that business's prospects—the stock market may be affected. With so many people trading on their own electronically, circumventing brokers and others who might demand harder evidence beyond a news release or news story, the effects of Web-carried releases can be substantial. Add unscrupulous motives to the mix and a real danger exists that the Web will be used to manipulate stock prices and investors' behavior.

Traditionally, news releases reach the public only after passing through the filter of the news media. Journalists scrutinize the material, challenge it when appropriate, and then report whatever they deem newsworthy. Making those releases directly available to the public replaces that system with something very different: unmediated media. Journalists now must figure out how to monitor that avenue of communication.

Whether the focus is on traditional media or new media, the electronic global village is still under construction. The Internet carries forward the process begun by radio and television. It increases the number of avenues along which real-time news can travel.

The rise of the Internet challenges journalists to reconsider their roles and responsibilities as providers of information to the public. If they fail to do so, they may find themselves increasingly irrelevant, left behind by a new generation of communicators (who might or might not call themselves "journalists"). Anyone who sets up a Web site will be able to disseminate "news" quickly and inexpensively to a potential audience of millions. Will Matt Drudge become the Walter Lippmann or Walter Cronkite of this new information universe? Mainstream journalists may shudder at that prospect, but this is a Wild West period for communications. A new egalitarian medium is here, and "going live" will happen constantly.

THE EVOLUTION OF LIVE

When Marshall McLuhan coined the term "global village," it was seen as a clever oxymoron that nicely captured television's capabilities. The medium would make the remote seem proximate. Events from throughout the world would appear with electronic vividness, as if they were happening just down the street from the viewer's home. With the globe thus shrunk, diverse peoples could become a cohesive community.

The technology may work superbly, but the sociology is not so simple. Distant happenings might become more comprehensible thanks to television, but they still remain foreign, literally and figuratively. The audience takes note of the many wars and disasters (and, occasionally, less depressing happenings) that constitute the news, but viewers' emotional and intellectual connections to the people directly affected by these events usually remain tenuous.

After all, television is confined to a glass box. No matter how gruesome the scenes on the screen may be, no blood will spill onto the carpet. No matter how close television seems to bring the day's events, they always remain distant enough to be viewed with dispassion. The global village can be visited and abandoned at will.

IN THE BEGINNING, RADIO

On November 2, 1920, Pittsburgh radio station KDKA reported election results to its listeners. Two years later, New York's WEAF carried the first broadcast advertisement. In 1924, Americans spent more than $350 million on radio sets.

Much of early radio was live: vaudeville acts, music from hotel ballrooms, play-by-play sports coverage, and news. Politicians, most notably Franklin Roosevelt, discovered that radio let them establish an unprecedented relationship with their constituents by entering their living rooms electronically.

Radio news could deliver a powerful, dramatic punch. The fiery end of the dirigible *Hindenburg* in 1937 was reported with great emotion by a radio correspondent on the scene. (This was recorded and broadcast later, the first instance of recorded material being so used.)[12] The effects of radio news on public opinion were evident in the months prior to America's entry into World War II. Edward R. Murrow, broadcasting from Britain during the Nazi blitz, vividly described the plight of friends under siege. His reports—which he began, "This is London"—gave Americans their first "living room war": the sounds of air-raid

sirens, antiaircraft fire, and German bombs; the click of London-
ers' footsteps on battered sidewalks; the eerie silence that hung
in the air until the next wave of bombers arrived. Americans listened and responded to war, not as political exercise but as
human drama. A Gallup poll in September 1940 found that only
16 percent of Americans favored providing more aid to Britain.
A month later, with the devastating effects of the blitz better
known—thanks in large part to Murrow—that number had risen
to 52 percent.

Radio journalism flourished during World War II, particularly at CBS with the team assembled by Murrow. Soon thereafter, television captured Americans' interest, and Murrow and
many of his radio colleagues moved into the new medium. Even
today, however, radio remains a primary source of news (particularly during the endless rush-hour "drive times").

From its earliest days, television journalism emphasized
speed. "Today's news today!" was the slogan of NBC News
when it began its first television newscast in 1949. During the
next decade, television's role in American life expanded rapidly
(much as the Internet is doing today). By the 1960s, the medium
was mature enough to be depended on in times of crisis.

TWO FUNERALS

Sometimes television pulls together an audience so vast that
the globe actually seems to shrink to the size of McLuhan's village. This happened notably for two funerals, which much of the
world (or at least much of the television-owning world) watched
as they took place. Live coverage allowed viewers to be more
than distant observers. They felt themselves to be real-time participants in the stories as they unfolded.

In 1963, television was emerging from adolescence, especially in the United States. More than 90 percent of American

households owned a TV set. Three years earlier, television had taken a significant step in its transformation of politics. Televised debates between presidential contenders underscored the need for candidates to possess on-camera skills. John Kennedy's appreciation of the medium's demands and power helped him win the White House. As president, he used live news conferences to enhance his political stature. But after a tenure of little more than a thousand days, he was assassinated.

In 1963, the country was unprepared for such trauma. Within the next two decades, Americans would see enough domestic turmoil to desensitize them. Two more national political leaders would be murdered; two presidents would survive assassination attempts; riots, scandals, and a distant war would strip away any vestiges of civic innocence. But in 1963, disbelief and confusion greeted the news of Kennedy's death.

That news first reached many people via television. Afternoon soap operas were interrupted by a picture of a card reading "News Bulletin" and a terse voice-over report of shots being fired at the presidential motorcade in Dallas. Then came the anchormen, shocked but composed, delivering the somber news of the president's death.

The nation was being informed of a national event. People did not have to wait until newspapers could be printed, and they did not have to settle for disembodied radio voices. The story did not ripple across the country, spread by local news organizations or word of mouth. Through the national television networks, news of Kennedy's death hit every part of America quickly and simultaneously. Americans could see a patchwork of images—incomplete but still strangely reassuring—that made tragedy more tangible.

Television's task on this occasion extended beyond providing sporadic bulletins. Network coverage of the funeral and other elements of the assassination's aftermath acted as a unifying force. ABC News president Elmer Lower later wrote:

Television held this nation together for four days, keeping people informed by a steady flow of news, and showing them vividly that President Johnson had taken command of the situation and that the transfer of power had taken place smoothly. . . . The steady flow of news gave a sense of confidence.[13]

The assassination occurred on a Friday, and during that weekend NBC spent seventy-one hours covering related events, ABC sixty, and CBS fifty-five.[14] The public responded with rapt attention. The A. C. Nielsen rating service reported that the average home in their viewing sample watched more than thirty-one hours of the coverage. Approximately 166 million Americans in more than 51 million homes were watching.[15] (In 1963, the U.S. population was slightly more than 180 million, with roughly 54 million households.) When the funeral procession began, 93 percent of American TV sets were tuned in to the coverage.[16]

Substantial parts of the coverage simply put the viewing audience at the scene. NBC, for example, broadcast throughout the night, showing a live shot from the Capitol Rotunda of crowds filing past the coffin. "For six hours," wrote NBC News president Reuven Frank, "nothing was heard but feet shuffling, coughing, guards changing, some whispering, an announcer every hour, for five seconds."[17]

Although most of the audience was American, parts of the rest of the world were able to watch excerpts of the weekend's events. The Telstar satellite had carried its first broadcasts in 1962, and the Kennedy coverage was fed by NBC via the Relay satellite. Television historian Mary Ann Watson wrote that in NBC's New York studio "eight European reporters narrated the picture transmission in their own languages. And for the first time, satellite relays reached beyond the Iron Curtain."[18] Parts of the coverage reached twenty-three other countries, with populations totaling more than 600 million people.

Given the nature of their equipment and the lack of time to plan, the networks grappled successfully, for the most part, with the technical demands of so much live coverage. While the funeral proceeded at its stately pace in Washington, further developments in Dallas tested the networks' resources. As suspected assassin Lee Harvey Oswald was about to be transferred from the city to the county jail, he was fatally shot by nightclub owner Jack Ruby. NBC was the only network that happened to be showing the scene from the jail.

Although the entire story of this weekend was rooted in a violent act, this was the first time that violence related to the assassination was carried live. NBC's audience did not merely hear a report about what had occurred and did not even have to wait for film to be shown after the fact. They saw the shooting of Oswald as it happened.

For television policy makers, events in Dallas presented difficult choices about what to show their audiences. The assassination of the president had been captured by a home movie camera owned by Abraham Zapruder. It was shocking footage that showed the president's head exploding as the bullets struck him. ABC and NBC decided that it was too graphic to air. Meanwhile, *Life* magazine purchased Zapruder's film and eventually published it as a series of still photographs. (CBS explored the possibility of renting the film from *Life*, but the magazine refused.)[19]

With time to ponder the likely impact of Zapruder's film, television executives backed off. Live coverage, however, was seen as a different matter in regard to viewers' sensitivities. An NBC producer, asked later by a researcher what he thought about broadcasting the Oswald shooting live, said:

> I thought it was great. Not the same feelings of taste as having the President shot; it wasn't gory. I would have stayed with it. I think if we had been live, I'd have stayed with the

President too; when it's live you have no control and the judgments differ because of that.[20]

This is an early example of the dichotomy that exists in decision making about content: What is deemed unacceptable in a filmed or taped story may be tolerated (or even valued) in live coverage. Having "no control" may be offered as justification for airing material that would otherwise be challenged.

Beyond these issues, the 1963 Kennedy assassination and funeral coverage is considered by many to have been one of television's finest moments, not so much for its reportorial content as for its helping to weld individual Americans' feelings into a national grieving. Americans suddenly had something new in common. They were seeing the same images in their homes, and they were sharing the resulting surge of emotion. This produced a common sense of loss.

This coverage also contributed much to the Kennedy mystique. Journalists Robert J. Donovan and Ray Scherer wrote:

> The president who flew to Texas four days previously to strengthen his political standing was by no means a legendary figure. It was on the scores of millions of television screens in America and around the world that the legend of John Fitzgerald Kennedy was born in the 75 hours between Dealey Plaza and Arlington National Cemetery.[21]

Thirty-four years later, another funeral similarly illustrated the technological and emotional reach of live television. When Diana, Princess of Wales, was killed in an automobile accident, television again became a unifying force. Convulsive grief in Britain and elsewhere was fueled by the extensive television coverage that allowed a worldwide audience to participate—as viewers—in Diana's funeral.

British newspapers estimated the worldwide TV audience at about 2.5 billion. British television was joined by American and other networks in covering the event. CNN provided seven hours of live funeral coverage and replayed the funeral service itself twice within twenty-four hours to accommodate time differences in the 210 countries and 600 broadcasting affiliates it served. Since John Kennedy's death, access to such events had dramatically increased due to the pervasiveness of television throughout the world and the steadily increasing sophistication and affordability of satellite technology.

Television and radio were not alone in providing live coverage following Diana's death. A new medium made its presence felt. Internet Web sites quickly posted reports about the accident and provided biographical information about the princess, in some cases delivering product faster than television did. Merrill Brown, editor in chief of MSNBC on the Internet, said, "We need to recognize that the Web has arrived. You could advance your knowledge much more by going into the Web."[22]

Compared with television, the Internet has a small audience. ABC News, for example, recorded 2 million page views during the day before and day of Diana's funeral. That may not be many when compared with the number of television viewers, but it indicates that people were starting to use the Internet as a supplier of news. In this case, this audience was presumably turning to Web sites as supplements to, rather than replacements for, other media. That will change as Web technology improves.

Television does a good job—at least in the technical sense—of covering grand events such as state funerals. The generals of TV news know how to deploy their troops. The BBC used more than 100 cameras for the twelve straight hours of coverage that it devoted to Diana's funeral. Editorial content, however, is often not as distinguished, with much that is inane and maudlin. Simply showing events unfold, accompanied by silence from the journalists, would be better, but of course the anchors and other TV newspeople are not paid huge salaries to be silent.

A polished solemnity imbues reports about the death of a national or world figure. Journalists are somberly respectful, regardless of how they treated the person while alive. The public usually absorbs these messages and reflects this mood, encouraged as well as united in grief by the mass media.

WHEN ANGER SUPERSEDES GRIEF

Sometimes, however, the public responds very differently. Anger can transcend grief. In such instances, live coverage can have an incendiary, not soothing, effect. Public sentiment may quickly set its own pace and direction, regardless of the tone and substance of the news coverage.

This was visible in April 1968, when Martin Luther King Jr. was assassinated in Memphis. As the news flashed around the country, the speed of the story's delivery was matched by the speed of the public's response, especially in America's heavily African-American inner cities. Civil disorders began in a few cities and were televised, and soon many more riots broke out. About this phenomenon, media scholar Erik Barnouw wrote that the electronic media collectively "sorts and distributes information, igniting memories. . . . The impulses it transmits can stir the juices of emotion and can trigger action. As in the case of a central nervous system, aberrations can deeply disturb the body politic."[23] The event was followed by a televised melange of images: the president addressing the nation; footage of King marching at Selma and speaking at the Lincoln Memorial; clips of police chasing looters and officials appealing for order and clergy invoking King's avowals of nonviolence. It is a jumble of sights and sounds, coming quickly but not always clearly, mediated by the journalist narrators who sound authoritative.

In the aftermath of King's death, there were riots in 110 cities. Thirty-nine people were killed (most of them black) and 2,500 were injured. More than 75,000 National Guardsmen and federal troops patrolled America's urban centers.[24] This was not a nation "united in grief," as it seemed to be after John Kennedy's death. It was, rather, a nation torn by a grief that engendered anger as well as mourning. Television itself did not cause that tear, but it may have been one of the instruments of it. When added to already volatile conditions, news coverage that emphasized speed over context proved dangerously potent.

King's assassination was just one event in a horrific year that later saw the murder of Robert Kennedy and battles between demonstrators and police in Chicago during the Democratic National Convention. Meanwhile, the war in Southeast Asia became bloodier. Television was there for it all, letting Americans see tragic events as they happened or shortly thereafter.

THE NUMBING OF THE AUDIENCE

Unlike the anger that it exhibited after King's murder, the public received news of Robert Kennedy's death with a numb passivity. Television news exhibited what was becoming a patterned response. Besides providing the finite amount of useful information, journalists rushed to supply every morsel of "news" that met the most liberal definition of relevance. Reuven Frank wrote of the coverage of Robert Kennedy's murder:

> The turmoil at a time like this cannot be imagined by laity, who know only their human, private puzzlement. We in news have that, too, but it is submerged by our obsessive need to be doing something, anything, fulfilling our roles, acting out how we see ourselves. Bystanders are corralled and bullied into telling what they saw. People still in shock

are thrust before cameras. Rational thought is a luxury as reporters and production associates race to get anyone at all
before a camera, while directors move cameras to where they
can get a picture worth showing and producers scream that
we need new material.[25]

Looking at this same scene, Michael Arlen, television critic for
The New Yorker, wrote:

> He was shot and it was real—a life, a death, the *event*, confu-
> sion, motion, people running, the man on the floor, young
> girls in straw hats crying, policemen, people pushing, yell-
> ing, the man on the floor, dying, dead, dying. It was all there
> for a moment, for a short while (it is perhaps this moment,
> stretching out forward and backward in our imaginations,
> that now remains), this event, this God knows what it was,
> and then the hands of people began to touch it. Inevitably,
> one will say. Inevitably.[26]

The inevitable touching that Arlen cites is what TV news
does. The handlers of tragedy are the reporters and commenta-
tors who massage and stroke and pummel the event, squeezing
out whatever they can. They fill their allotted airtime with a mix
of news and truth (not always the same thing), fact and innu-
endo, journalism and philosophizing. They condemn the accused gunman and then offer a halfhearted disclaimer that "of
course, he's innocent until proven guilty." They ask predictable
questions that elicit predictable answers. They talk about irony,
apparently without understanding what the word means. They
become ever more ponderous, their pace and content increasingly lugubrious. Arlen called this "griefspeak." It is journalism
colored by self-indulgence.

Television can carry much information, but there are limits
to the amount of weight it can support. The structure of television news wobbles when subjected to an unusually heavy load.

Perhaps viewers have come to expect too much of TV news in terms of bearing the tribulations of society on its shoulders, assuming that it will be Atlas for the modern world. But television journalists themselves have done little to reduce expectations about their role as glorified messengers.

ENTERTAINMENT AND POLITICS

Beyond its journalistic role, live television occasionally demonstrates its enormous reach by pulling together a vast audience for certain sports and entertainment events. The World Cup final match is watched by more than 3 billion viewers worldwide. Taped material also can draw huge audiences. In the United States, the final episode of a program such as *M.A.S.H.* or *Seinfeld* will attract more than 100 million viewers. In 1999, Barbara Walters's interview with Monica Lewinsky—a session that was part news, part freak show—attracted half the nation's television audience. With a 33.4 rating, it was seen in approximately 33 million American households.

Sliding back into journalism, live television has brought its entertainment values to politics, enhancing the drama of election nights and candidate debates. Election night embarrassment, such as that created for the *Chicago Tribune* by its 1948 DEWEY DEFEATS TRUMAN headline, is not much of a concern now. The networks' exit polling and computer models work so well that their accuracy is taken for granted. The principal questions that network producers must answer are about timing. Is the basic journalistic responsibility to deliver the news as soon as it is available, or should other issues—such as the potential impact of early projections on voter turnout—be considered? News organizations try to have it both ways. They try to be the first to get results to the public while disclaiming any interference with the voting process.

In the 1980 presidential election, for example, NBC flashed "Reagan Wins" on-screen at 8:15 P.M. Eastern time, while voting was still going on in one third of the states in the Central time zone and in every state farther west. President Jimmy Carter then made his concession speech at 9:50 P.M. Eastern time, while voting was still under way in most of the Pacific time zone states.

The timing of these announcements made no difference in the presidential race, since Carter was being soundly defeated. But some congressional and local races were much closer. Lines of voters reportedly melted away after the network projections and Carter's speech. Who left in greater numbers—exultant Republicans or discouraged Democrats—cannot be determined, but in a nation with consistently miserable voter participation, anything that depresses turnout deserves scrutiny. Granted, Carter's early concession had to be covered live, but news organizations can decide for themselves on most election days when to deliver their projections.

In congressional testimony in 1981, CBS News president William Leonard said:

> We believe our responsibility is . . . to report accurately the information we have, and its significance, as soon as it becomes available. . . . We cannot patronize our audience by withholding from them what we know. To do so would be a violation of trust and would seriously jeopardize our credibility.[27]

Leonard's remarks sound virtuous but are a bit disingenuous. The networks are happy to tape-delay events such as Olympic competition when it serves their interest. They observe embargoes on certain items, and they withhold important news stories (such as those involving national security concerns) when they believe the public interest is best served by doing so.

On the other hand, being coy about how an election is turning out also has its problems. By 1992, the networks had pooled their research resources, so all had the same data on which to base projections. Although Ross Perot conceded at 10:30 P.M. Eastern time, the networks did not declare Bill Clinton the winner until about twenty minutes later. Soon thereafter, George Bush conceded and about an hour later Bill Clinton appeared at his Little Rock victory celebration.

The *New York Times* editorialized that "the four networks deserve unstinting praise for threading a careful path between sensationalism and censorship." But Michael Kinsley, writing in *Time*, disagreed: "The drama that had you glued to your TV was a fraud perpetrated by a vast conspiracy [of journalists and politicians who knew exactly] what everyone else was waiting to hear, yet pretended ignorance. . . . The networks generated false tension while suppressing the very information that would dissipate it." Kinsley also pointed out that by the time many West Coast voters are casting their ballots, the election *has* been decided, regardless of whether the results have been reported on television.[28]

Yet another judgment was offered in 1992 by the Committee for the Study of the American Electorate, a nonpartisan research organization, which sponsored the following newspaper ad:

> Early projections are bad journalism. The news on election night is the actual tally of the ballots cast. What the networks report on election night—projections based on their exit polls and/or sample precinct analyses—is not the news but their own contrivances.

The ad urged the networks to agree not to project results in any race in which people were still voting.

Such restraint is unlikely to have much appeal for news organizations. Rather, they are accelerating the delivery of election returns by releasing them on Web sites that provide voting data as soon as it is available, even before it is digested and delivered over the air. News organizations will still face decisions about how much information to release and when to do so. During the 2000 presidential primaries, the networks' exit poll results—which give a good indication of the final outcome—were leaked to several Internet news providers early in the afternoon, many hours before all the polls closed. The *Drudge Report* and *Slate* posted those numbers, causing much harumphing by network executives who had vowed to avoid premature release. Despite protestations of their virtue, the networks used the exit polls during their early evening newscasts—again, before polls had closed—to report voter attitudes. The anchors and analysts did not specifically say who was going to win, but they provided enough information so anyone with the slightest knowledge of politics would know what the outcomes would probably be.

Campaign debates also have evolved to meet the demands of the dominant medium. When Abraham Lincoln debated Stephen Douglas throughout Illinois in their 1858 Senate race, both men spoke for hours, targeting their efforts at the audience on hand and those who would read about it in local newspapers. The modern era of candidate debates is generally considered to have begun with the face-off between John Kennedy and Richard Nixon on September 26, 1960. By allowing the entire nation to witness the live on-camera skills of the aspirants, presidential debates have established a new criterion for those who want to move into the White House: you *must* be good on television, or at least better than your opponent. (After a three-election lapse, these debates began again in 1976 and have been part of every presidential race since then. The gap was primarily attributable to the equal opportunity provision of the Communications Act of 1934. The clause was suspended by Congress during the 1960 campaign, and court rulings in 1975 and 1984 provided exemptions that allowed the debates to be limited to the major candidates.)

Perhaps all politics is theater. Live televised debates underscore the importance of acting as an element of campaigning. Debates are evaluated, at least by many journalists, not on the basis of *what* was said but *how* it was said. Performance is measured by self-appointed judges. Gaffes and clever one-liners take on lives of their own, replayed constantly on newscasts and sometimes in candidates' commercials. The politicians' appearance is appraised in purely television terms: Did their makeup run? Did they look tired or old or wooden or bored? Did they play to the cameras properly? Substance sometimes matters less than the illusion of substance.

Audiences for these debates know that they are seeing politics as show. Journalist Roger Simon has observed that "most people watch presidential debates for the same reason most people watch the Indy 500: to see who crashes and burns."[29]

Recognizing journalists' fascination with these superficial matters, political strategists place heavy emphasis on debate technique. In 1996, Bill Clinton's handlers designed a sophisticated preparation to make sure their candidate was ready to debate Bob Dole. The president was coached about his gestures and facial expressions. Rehearsals were videotaped and the tapes then carefully scrutinized by Clinton and his aides. The second of that year's two debates featured a town meeting format, with the candidates partly surrounded by the "average voters" who would question them. For this session, Clinton's movements on the stage had been precisely choreographed in ways designed to irritate Dole and look good on camera. Clinton was a diligent student. His debate coach, Michael Sheehan, said, "For me, working with Clinton is like Kazan getting to work with Brando."[30]

Dole, meanwhile, disdained rehearsals, believing that all his years as a master of debate in the U.S. Senate would prove to be more than adequate preparation. He was wrong. Mastery of the

Senate floor—even when the proceedings were carried live by C-SPAN—has little to do with mastering network prime time.

Although presidential candidates' television skills are endlessly analyzed by journalists as integral elements of campaigning, critics often dismiss them as indicators of likely performance in office. Governing, so the argument goes, requires far more substantive talents than does televised vote seeking. But such criticism overlooks the fact that the presidency itself has become in many ways television dependent. The skills necessary to "looking presidential" on television during a campaign are also necessary in an effective presidency.

In times of crisis, the televised address to the nation (and to the world) is an essential presidential tool. Just as a president's words are weighed, so too is his demeanor as it is conveyed over the airwaves. Some presidents, such as John Kennedy and Ronald Reagan, did well at this; others, such as Lyndon Johnson and Jimmy Carter, less so.

Kennedy's televised speech on October 22, 1962, at the height of the Cuban missile crisis, was a calm and forceful warning about the cataclysmic danger facing America and the world at that moment. Reagan's remarks on January 28, 1986, after the space shuttle *Challenger* exploded, also illustrated, on a smaller scale, the importance of a president using television to pull the country together. Reagan spoke for only a few minutes, but it was an essential and effective performance. In times of crisis, Americans now reflexively turn to television and expect to find their president there.

LIVING ROOM WAR

The Vietnam War has been called the "living room war" because it was the first war that television brought into American living rooms night after night, a descendant of the radio war delivered in the 1940s by Edward R. Murrow and others.

It is worth noting that none of the Vietnam coverage was live. There was live reporting during those years, but the satellite system was not yet complete enough to allow direct broadcasting from Vietnam. Film and tape had to be shipped from Saigon to Tokyo or another location where relay equipment was available.

The living room war made combat an intimate experience for those watching it at home. The *New Yorker*'s Michael Arlen wrote that on the TV screen "we were watching, a bit numbly perhaps (we have watched it so often), real men get shot at, real men (our surrogates, in fact) get killed and wounded." Viewers were close and yet removed, Arlen continued, watching the war "as a child, kneeling in a corridor, his eye to the keyhole, looks at two grownups arguing in a locked room—the aperture of the keyhole small; the figures shadowy, mostly out of sight; the voices indistinct."[31] Television provides and controls that keyhole view of war: episodic flashes devoid of context, blood that disappears when the channel is changed.

During the Vietnam War, what appeared on viewers' screens was still the product of the standard editorial process of TV news. After stories were written and edited, they could be examined by producers and other higher-ups to review accuracy, gore, and security concerns. Packaged stories were almost always at least twenty-four hours removed from the action, so a bit of additional time could be taken for in-house decision making about content.

By the start of the Persian Gulf War, that cushion of time was gone. In January 1991, the first bombing of Iraq began during America's network newscasts, which carried live audio reports about the air strike from correspondents in Baghdad.

Live coverage of war and other foreign policy crises brings with it some difficult ethical problems. When governments use the news media as messengers, the key word is "use." Political purposes do not always conform to journalistic standards. For example, the governments' messages might not be truthful; they may be nothing more than disinformation, carefully crafted to serve the source's interests. By providing a clear channel for their dissemination, news organizations become mere conveyer belts. Editorial judgments about accuracy are sacrificed, and journalists become purveyors of *news*, which is not necessarily *truth*.

This distinction is important. A pronouncement from Saddam Hussein, Vladimir Putin, an American president, or another world leader is news if it meets a threshold test of importance. But determining its truthfulness requires a different and far more challenging test. News organizations must decide if their responsibility is to deliver merely the news or to report only the truth. Particularly because of time pressures that may prevent verification, live coverage inherently tilts toward news rather than truth.

Television's reporting of the Gulf War was an example of saturation coverage. Analyst Robert Lichter notes that there were "more television news stories in a shorter period of time" than for any other event in television's history. From August 2, 1990, through February 27, 1991, ABC, CBS, and NBC broadcast 4,383 Gulf-related stories on their evening newscasts, with a total airtime of 126 hours, 29 minutes. (By comparison, the 1988 presidential campaign yielded only 2,301 stories during 22 months.)[32]

Live components of the Gulf War coverage got the most attention, but "liveness" in itself does not necessarily mean that breaking news is being reported. Former NBC News president Reuven Frank observed that "there isn't anything happening live except for some Scud attacks. What we're getting 'live' is briefings about events that are from 12 to 48 hours old. And reporters talking to each other 'live.' "[33] Going live just for the sake of going live may have little journalistic value. The practice may even lend itself to manipulation. During the Gulf War, for example, the Pentagon allowed live coverage of the briefings Frank cites, knowing that the "liveness" of the event would be irresistible to the networks. The content of these briefings, however, was largely self-serving, and the live coverage made it impossible for journalists to corroborate or analyze what was being said until later. The Pentagon's message was delivered directly to the public, with the networks' imprimatur but without their being able to *report* independently about the contents of that message.

The vividness of live war coverage clearly demands a sophisticated understanding of ethical issues on the part of those who provide such coverage. It also requires special attention from those who wage war. Going to war is a political decision that, in a democracy, requires public support. Cultivating that support will be influenced by what the public sees on their television screens.

To a certain extent, this is a legacy of the Vietnam War. Some in government point to coverage of the 1968 Tet offensive as an example of how misperception fostered by news coverage can undermine policy. Their argument goes something like this: Tet was portrayed by American news organizations as a major setback for the United States and its South Vietnamese allies. But in truth, the communist forces were the real losers, suffering heavy casualties, failing to hold the cities and towns they had seized, and not getting the popular uprising they had hoped the offensive would spark.

In retrospect, this case has some merit. At the time most journalists did not recognize that the communists had failed to achieve their goals. But the coverage was accurate in the sense that the enemy's ability to launch a major offensive undermined the Johnson administration's claims that the war was going well and that the "light at the end of the tunnel"—a successful end to the war—was in view. Tet was a political defeat for the United States, if not truly a military one.

Whatever the news media's role in the problems of the Johnson presidency, later presidents have carefully considered news reports' impact on public opinion during military action. In the years preceding the Gulf War, journalists had to struggle with White House and Pentagon officials to gain access to small-scale intervention in Grenada and Panama. In these cases, the Reagan and Bush administrations were determined to limit coverage that might have undermined public support of their efforts. From the policy maker's standpoint, live coverage, with its more vivid drama, makes such controls even more important.

WHAT THE WORLD SEES

Journalism consists of more than news providers delivering information to news consumers. The news is not just a simple, tangible product that can be handed over and that's the end of it. News has effect, whether it is the nightmare a television viewer suffers after seeing a grisly news story, a massive demonstration by tens of thousands of news watchers protesting a government policy that the news media have analyzed, or still other thousands celebrating an event that news coverage has brought into their lives. Solid journalism—good writing, good pictures, good sound—will engage its audience, who will think and respond once the news is presented.

This thinking and responding constitute the true product of journalism, and they make professional responsibility an essential part of the journalist's job. That seems simple enough, but the news business is complicated by economic imperatives, technological factors, and audience expectations (real or perceived) that can obstruct the path toward consistently responsible news gathering and presentation. Most journalists operate in good faith, but sometimes they may be tripped up by these obstructions. Taking time to think about the news and its ramifications is the best way to avoid such missteps. Live coverage, however, reduces—and sometimes obliterates—that precious resource of time. Figuring out how to deal with this temporal compression is one of the most important tasks facing a news business that is increasingly going live.

2

THE ALLURE AND
IMPACT OF LIVE

L ive coverage is attractive to television and radio news executives partly because it gives electronic journalism a competitive edge over its print counterparts. Reporting a story as it
happens, rather than after the fact, is presumed to have innate
audience appeal because witnessing an exciting event is exciting
in itself. Later chapters will address the Internet's potential to
become the great equalizer by extending the ability to provide
real-time reports to print news organizations as well. But until
the Internet becomes more pervasive and its news delivery more
sophisticated, live coverage will remain dominated by television
and radio.

Speed is assumed to compensate for superficiality. That
may be a dangerous notion, but it has some resonance among
electronic news professionals, who frequently hear their product
dismissed as a headline service. The format of the standard
newscast is marked by its terseness and brisk pace, which means
that background and analysis are often squeezed out. Even an
all-news network such as CNN spends much of its time repeating stories instead of expanding on them. Newspapers and news
magazines can appeal to audiences by putting stories in context
(although they do not always do so), and they can advertise
themselves as providers of substance. Rather than argue endlessly about the relative intellectual heft of their respective offer-

ings, those who do television and radio news stress capabilities that print cannot match. The ability not only to deliver information but also to take the audience to the scene of events is an asset that television and radio networks and stations market assiduously. It is seen as a technique that can bolster audience interest, and thus ratings and revenue. A 1998 audience survey conducted by Frank N. Magid Associates, a leading research and consulting firm used by broadcasters, asked what local television stations could do to make viewers more interested in watching local news. The respondents' first choice was live coverage of stories going on at the moment.[1]

Findings such as those reported by Magid are common in the television business. They are important factors in stations' decisions about how to do their job and how to spend their money. Helicopters, satellite trucks, remote vans, and other tools of the live coverage trade soak up large amounts of local stations' budgets. Vans with microwave transmitters (for relatively short-range assignments) cost close to $250,000. Trucks that can feed material via satellite are about $500,000. Helicopters cost upward of $1 million. Not surprisingly, once those investments are made, managers are determined to put their expensive high-tech tools to use. An empty warehouse engulfed in vivid flames may make a perfect helicopter shot and lead a local newscast, regardless of there being no danger to people or other property. It's picturesque and it's live, so it's news.

Live coverage as a ratings getter can override more traditional journalistic matters, sometimes creating tension between news directors and reporters. A 1997 study found that news directors were less concerned than reporters about the impact of overused live coverage on the credibility of a station's news operations. Reporters were quicker to cite concerns about fact-checking being hindered by demands that they report live and fast. Nevertheless, the prevailing belief among the news directors and reporters surveyed for this study was that live reporting does attract viewers.[2] In most newsrooms, that is the controlling issue. The same study found that news directors and reporters "believe 'live for the sake of live' is a common practice in newsrooms across the country. . . . and that much of it is gratuitous live reporting, with no apparent journalistic justification."[3]

LIVE, LOCAL, AND LATE BREAKING

One of the most popular live stories is the car chase. This became a staple of TV news in 1994 with the O.J. Simpson low-speed chase prior to his arrest. Approximately 95 million people watched all or part of the Simpson pursuit, which was a perfect story for helicopter coverage.

Local stations with helicopters now regularly scramble when they hear reports of a chase on police radio. The people involved and the cause of the chase are irrelevant. What matters is the stations' ability to generate live reports about purported news that features drama and movement. For the viewers at home, this can be much like a video game as they watch the fleeing driver and his or her pursuers weave or, preferably, crash through traffic. All that's missing is a computer game joystick to allow the viewer to control the action.

Another favorite story for live coverage is the arrival of large numbers of police officers in response to a real or suspected crime. This kind of event is often perfect for a mix of aerial and on-the-ground reporting, particularly when a SWAT team rolls in with its heavy equipment. The helicopter can capture the scope of the deployment, with the flashing police lights and the officers on the move, while the reporter at the scene provides breathless description and maybe an interview or two. Perhaps the story is truly important—a hostage taking, for instance. Or perhaps it is a false alarm. No matter, the choreography and the resulting pictures are virtually the same.

Whether the subject of coverage is a warehouse fire, police raid, or other such event, the problem for serious journalists is the relegation of news judgment to a secondary status while technological capabilities become determinative. The theory in many newsrooms seems to be that if it's happening now and we can get live pictures, then it's newsworthy. Because of the uncertainty of outcome, live coverage may be intrinsically interesting, but importance tends to get lost in the rush to go live. As Ted Koppel has said, "The technological tail is wagging the editorial dog."[4]

This rearrangement of priorities that overemphasizes the trivial often means presenting a distorted picture to news consumers. The news of the day appears to consist of a series of spectacularly picturesque events, stunning in their immediacy but empty in their longer-term implications. This is television news at its show biz worst, falsely assigning significance to inconsequential happenings. As portrayed by this kind of coverage, the world looks like an action movie, with fires, car chases, SWAT teams on the move, victims howling, villains snarling, and so on. Viewers are likely to react with mixed excitement and fear. Most important, they are likely to keep watching.

Of course, the world is *not* an action movie, and most newscast viewers will find that their lives are untouched by the thrilling, frightening tales they see unfolding on the screen. If they stop to think about it, they will realize this (and be thankful). But if they watch enough of this kind of coverage, they may begin to see their world through a distorted lens. If madmen are being chased along the highway, perhaps it is not safe to drive. If so many crimes are being committed on the streets, maybe it would be wise just to stay home (and buy some new locks and a gun or two) and watch the evils of the world on television, viewing them electronically but also staying safely removed from the dangers they pose.

How the public reacts to the cumulative messages of news

may or may not be the responsibility of news organizations. On the one hand, if the stories being broadcast are accurate, then the journalists have done their job and it is up to the viewers to decide for themselves how much importance to attach to the news. On the other hand, if depictions of community life have been skewed by news organizations' sensation-oriented coverage, and if news consumers are reacting to this version of "reality," then journalists may bear some responsibility for that reaction. If, for example, disproportionate coverage (live and otherwise) of crime produces disproportionate fear of crime among audience members, can journalists simply shrug that off? "Let the viewer beware" is a convenient response, but it may be an ethical cop-out.

The newsworthiness debate, therefore, proceeds on several levels. On one, the concern is about covering events that may be interesting but are relatively unimportant and may squeeze out coverage of more significant matters. On another, the issue is the quantity of coverage, particularly when news consumers are being told—explicitly or implicitly—that the topic at hand is more important than it really is.

At the root of these problems is the fixation on "spot news," that is, a breaking story. Spot news is unpredictable, and a sudden twist in the story may catch journalists and their viewers unprepared. Since there is no time for exercising editorial judgment in real-time reporting, the out-of-control event roars wildly into the audience's living rooms.

An example of this occurred in Los Angeles in 1998. An armed man shut down a freeway shortly before rush hour, pointing a gun at passing cars and firing several rounds (hitting no one). As the police arrived at the scene, so did local television news crews, on the ground and in the air. While the standoff proceeded, six local stations and national cable channel MSNBC carried at least part of the event live, two of them interrupting after-school children's programming to do so. Finally, the man propped a shotgun under his chin and pulled the trigger.

Coverage of this event provoked the usual reaction: protests from viewers, apologies from the stations, and more debate about the perilous nature of live reporting. Los Angeles station KNBC (which is owned by NBC) issued a statement, saying, "We did not anticipate this man's actions in time to cut away, and we deeply regret that any of our viewers saw this tragedy on our air."[5] KNBC reported that it received 2,000 complaints and called each person back to apologize.[6]

Some news managers see such incidents as inevitable when stations are engaged in fierce competition to be first with on-the-spot reporting. Warren Cereghino, executive producer for Chris-Craft Television News Service, owner of Los Angeles station KCOP, which carried the suicide, said, "It was bound to happen. Any time you cover something live and unedited you're taking a risk." Jeff Wald, news director at Warner Bros. affiliate KTLA pointed out that at least part of the story needed to be covered: "You have a rush hour where 250,000 people were affected by somebody who was shooting at people on the freeway. That's a news story. Part of our duty is to warn people."[7]

Wald's comment underscores the dilemma TV news managers face. The ratings battle among stations is fought partly by trying to be first at every story in which viewers might be interested. (This is particularly true in an intensely competitive market such as Los Angeles.) The public has come to expect live coverage of breaking stories and presumably will change channels to find the most up-to-the-minute reporting. Even suggestions about using a five-second delay when covering events that could become bloody are viewed with wariness by some in the television news business. They do not want to lag even five seconds behind competitors who might choose not to delay. None of the local news directors said they would stop live coverage of freeway chases or other dangerous events, only that they would try to avoid airing violent conclusions of those events.

Howard Rosenberg of the *Los Angeles Times* showed little patience with such policies, writing,

> They'll never admit it—perhaps not even to themselves—but Thursday was the day Los Angeles television stations finally got what they wanted. . . . This time it was the full payoff, the big public splatter, the full shotgun-to-the-head kablooie. And you and your children, Southern California, were able to see it live. . . . It represents the ultimate horror of the kind of live coverage that is increasingly practiced everywhere. No safety nets. No editing process. No control, just a total abrogation of journalistic responsibility.[8]

For this kind of story the debate centers on two basic issues. *How* to cover gets the most attention, but *whether* to cover may be the more difficult question. The first can be addressed with technical changes such as tape delay and using wide shots instead of close-ups, and finally cutting away quickly when a bloody moment appears about to occur. But being too cautious about whether an event is worth covering can conflict with a fundamental journalistic task. Walter Goodman of the *New York Times* wrote about the Los Angeles suicide coverage:

> Journalism has never been a particularly fastidious line of work; that's part of its value and appeal. It is by its nature intrusive and in constant search of excitement. . . . Journalists have their opportunities to be do-gooders and arbiters of taste, but not at the expense of suppressing news.

In the rush of delivering daily television news, noted Goodman, the best rule is, "When in doubt, cover and carry."[9]

Along similar lines, Cheryl Fair, news director at KABC in Los Angeles, said:

The technology has progressed to the point that it allows the viewer to see more of the process of gathering news. . . . People are seeing news as it develops. And I'm not sure that's bad. It kind of hits at some of the criticism of the media for slanting the news. You can't say it was slanted when it's live.[10]

Perhaps live reporting is, as Fair suggested, a purer form of journalism. Or perhaps that rationale is merely a way to avoid making tough editorial decisions. Even if news coverage is supposed to mirror what has happened or is happening, journalists must decide where to place the mirror. Failure to exercise thoughtful control over the positioning of the mirror and the delivery of the image it captures means providing a product that is "unedited" in the word's truest sense.

To take this point a step farther, an argument can be made that at least some live coverage is not really journalism at all. It is voyeurism. Journalism is a process: gathering information, analyzing its veracity and importance, acquiring supplemental information, and then putting it in an understandable, useful form for delivery to the public. Live coverage can short-circuit that process, going from gathering to delivery with nothing in between. This may use the technological tools of modern journalism, but it is not necessarily journalism itself.

The Los Angeles suicide coverage was not an isolated case. Just a month later another Los Angeles freeway incident presented news stations with the same kind of problem. A driver—later identified as a Los Angeles police officer distraught about personal matters—led police on a chase before apparently intentionally driving her car into a freeway piling, killing herself. One station carried the chase and crash live; others used tape of it on their newscasts.[11]

Many stations around the country continue to get caught up in the drama of chases and other spot news. Presented with reporters' attention-grabbing breathlessness, real or feigned, these stories have become the stylistic trademarks of some local television news operations.

BEYOND LOCAL

Live journalism is by no means limited to spot news. Substantive stories also may lend themselves to live coverage, requiring more than superficial reporting. Live coverage of major stories illustrates the conflicts between speed and depth, and the problems that arise when the latter is sacrificed in pursuit of the former.

Television is increasingly relied upon as the source of continuous information about an ongoing story. But not all television networks perform this role in the same way. CNN has made this its signature style of operation, creating a difficult choice for other news organizations. To play CNN's game requires a substantial commitment of personnel, money, and hardware, as well as a willingness to let news stories sometimes override non-news programming at the risk of chasing away a substantial part of the audience. For example, while CNN might as a matter of course provide a live update of a story of even passing importance at 10:30 P.M. Eastern time on a Thursday, NBC presumably would be very hesitant to break into its top-rated *E.R.* to cover anything less significant than the end of the world. CBS and ABC are in much the same situation, and along with NBC have ceded territory to CNN.

A lot of this territory lies outside the United States. As of late 1998, CNN had twenty-three foreign bureaus with correspondents, while ABC had five, CBS four, and NBC (with its sibling MSNBC) seven. Newcomer Fox had five.[12] Despite this apparent imbalance, the "big three" are not abandoning international coverage. They do, however, rely increasingly on their partnerships with foreign networks, such as Japan's NHK and Germany's ZDF, plus international television news agencies such as Reuters Television and Associated Press Television News. In addition to maintaining its own bureaus, CNN has two-way relationships with international partners, giving and receiving video.

This new mapping of news-gathering terrain is partly a function of the expanded number of news organizations that want what is often the same product. It is important to keep in mind that much of "the news" on any given day is not unique to the news organization that presents it. The rundowns of top stories on all the networks' newscasts often look strikingly similar; events that are newsworthy for one are probably newsworthy for the others. If a major story of the day is about Japan's economic situation, NHK can provide whatever video an American network would want. The hard information on which the story is based might be gathered by telephone or computer from a newsroom in the United States. Each network may end up with basically the same story that has been put together in much the same minimalist way.

For the network to have its own crew in Japan in this instance would not be cost-efficient. The story needs to be covered, but doing it through a partnership with a Japanese video provider would, in most instances, produce a story equal in quality to one that the network did entirely by itself. As this approach becomes more commonly accepted, reliance on partnerships will increase, perhaps to the point at which one of the "big three" contracts with CNN for substantial parts of overseas reporting.

This may make great financial sense, but questions arise about the journalistic content. The news will become a more homogeneous product: one size fits all. Enterprise reporting—the digging and scraping that produce scoops and insight—might become rare, replaced by yet another manifestation of pack journalism. This kind of generic coverage first defines and then reinforces the conventional wisdom about the topic at hand. Two potential problems arise from this: first, the public may get just a narrow view of a broad issue and, second, the conventional wisdom may be wrong.

The appeal of shared news gathering is not unique to foreign stories. Reliance on coverage partnerships is also increasing at home. Networks share exit polling on election day and use pool video when logistics or cost makes that desirable. The economics of this approach are so alluring that they may seem to offset the traditional value of self-reliance. That, however, may be an illusion. In journalism as in other businesses, competition can improve quality. Conversely, diminished competition may mean diminished quality.

When a major story breaks, partnerships usually give way to battling for unique story angles. The resulting news product, however, should not be regarded as merely a trophy by the competing journalists. Most important is the effect on the audience—how people use the information they receive.

IMPACT ON THE COMMUNITY

At 12:30 P.M. on March 24, 1998, at Westside Middle School in Jonesboro, Arkansas, the fire alarm sounded. As students filed out of the school, they were met by gunfire from a wooded area about 100 yards away. A teacher and four students were killed; ten other students were wounded. The shooters were quickly apprehended: two boys, aged thirteen and eleven.

Jonesboro, population 51,000, has only one television station, KAIT—an ABC affiliate and one of eight stations owned by Cosmos Broadcasting Corporation. A reporter and the station's one live truck were on the way to the school moments after hearing the first report of the shooting on the newsroom radio scanner. At 1:09, KAIT interrupted programming and an anchor reported that there had been a shooting at the school and that a number of people had been wounded. At 1:30, the station presented its first live report from the scene.

Several days of intensive local, regional, national, and even international television coverage followed. The ABC, CBS, and NBC nightly newscasts together devoted sixty-eight minutes to the story during the next five weekdays. The "big three" staffed their coverage with fifty-four people in Jonesboro (thirteen on-air and the rest support personnel). CNN, Fox, and foreign networks added sixty-four more staff members. Print news organizations were also there in force, led by the Associated Press and the *New York Times*, with seven people each. Altogether, about seventy news organizations sent more than 200 staff members to the small Arkansas city.[13]

Despite the intensive coverage by national news organizations, local television was probably most important to the people of Jonesboro. In an analysis written for a Freedom Forum study of the Jonesboro coverage, former CNN executive vice president Ed Turner said that KAIT's reports

> often were long on emotion, but they did not embarrass, mislead or inflame. In a sense, the station served as a place where the community could grieve and the newscasts undoubtedly were appreciated for their sensitive tone. . . . On a story like this, a moderate to high level of emotion is to be expected—and that is not necessarily bad for a community, a region or even a nation. Like KAIT in Jonesboro, the networks may have opened up a place of grieving to accommodate a national audience. Is that journalism? Insofar as human emotions are part of any tragedy, yes.[14]

This kind of coverage includes many elements, ranging from spot news reporting to background and analysis pieces that try to explain the hows and whys of the event. Live reporting must meet special standards in these circumstances. Responsibility extends to not only the general audience but also the subjects of coverage. In the Jonesboro story, television viewers did not have to be shielded from raw, graphic pictures, such as those of the Los Angeles freeway suicide. Like much live reporting, the coverage was after the fact in the sense that the key event itself—the shooting—was over and the victims had been removed by the time live coverage from the scene began, which was an hour after the gunfire. The KAIT reporter described the scene and the number of casualties. That is horrific enough, but at least the report did not include live pictures of the bloody victims.

Most of the live coverage in the Jonesboro story consisted of reporters who were at the school mainly to convey the sense of "being there." Other live reports included interviews with police officers, other officials, and witnesses, including children.

These latter interviews are the ones that should be done cautiously because they can so easily slip into being exploitative. Children (and most adults) have had no prior experience of being interviewed. Some television interviews are unlike normal conversations because the person being interviewed does not even see the people asking questions; he or she stares into a camera lens while the interviewers' words arrive through an earpiece. After a tragedy, it is easy to become emotional or say something that may cause embarrassment later. The questions themselves may exacerbate post-trauma stress. An experienced interviewer, however, can proceed gently and minimize the chances of this happening. According to the Freedom Forum's study of the Jonesboro coverage, interviews with Westside students on ABC's *Good Morning America* and NBC's *Today* were handled carefully.

Another aspect of live reporting of such a story that sometimes is overlooked is the importance of the coverage to the local community. Television news can stop rumors before they spread and can serve as a bulletin board to let viewers know what is happening and how they might help. In Jonesboro, KAIT consistently provided prompt notice of memorial services, fund-raising efforts, and other community responses as the healing process began. Because of television, no resident of the area needed to fear being disconnected from what was going on.

Despite television journalists' generally positive efforts in Jonesboro, some reporters and photographers became overly aggressive. On several occasions when Westside students and their families came to the school gymnasium for the psychological counseling that was being offered, they found microphones and cameras thrust at them. On at least one occasion, several still photographers tried to take pictures through the window of a victim's house. (In response to that incident, the sheriff went to the press center and threatened to arrest anyone using such tactics.)

A story such as the Jonesboro shootings is filled with emotion and is certain to attract a large, rapt audience. It differs from the Los Angeles freeway story in its significance. The L.A. incident was tragic, as suicides always are. But there was only one victim, whereas in Jonesboro there were many. Also, the Jonesboro event forced people to come to grips with the frightening issue of children committing terrible acts as well as children being the victims of terrible acts. The seriousness of that issue may in itself conflict with the process of live news coverage. The *need* for live reports was limited by the fact that the deed was done, arrests had been made, and no one else was in danger. Live coverage was not needed to warn people about a continuing threat, as would have been the case if the assailants were at large and possibly attacking others.

The ability to warn of imminent danger—whether a gunman on the loose or a tornado on the ground—may be the most important role for live coverage of local stories. If such factors are not involved—if a true need to know is absent—different standards come into play. In the Jonesboro case, the story of the shooting itself could be covered conclusively and relatively tersely. The larger story was why it happened and what might be done to prevent such tragedies in the future. Addressing those issues requires far more than the reflexive journalism that characterizes much live reporting.

WHEN SUBSTANCE AND SENSATION COLLIDE

A presidency apparently headed toward impeachment is certainly a newsworthy story. But in the case of the Monica Lewinsky scandal that threatened to derail Bill Clinton's presidency, newsworthiness was mixed with salaciousness, creating difficulties for journalists. This was a particular problem when television news organizations wanted to offer live coverage, which meant that they were deprived of the time that would have allowed them to make editorial judgments about what was and what was not suitable to be aired.

When the report of independent counsel Kenneth Starr was released in September 1998, television news was the fervent messenger delivering it to the public. This was scarcely a high-tech presentation. On CBS, for example, reporter Bob Schieffer had his camera pull back to show three CBS staff members on the floor in front of him, scanning the report and handing it to him page by page as it emerged from a fax machine. The courtly Schieffer was obviously dismayed when encountering passages dealing with oral sex and other such fare that a congressional correspondent does not usually have to make part of his story. Schieffer did his best at on-the-spot editing and paraphrasing. Other networks and their reporters also proceeded with varying degrees of caution.

If not for the magnitude of the overall controversy, the collective performance could have been dismissed as merely another comic episode in television journalism's perpetual (although sometimes halfhearted) struggle to reconcile "news" and "taste." The larger question in covering the release of the Starr report, however, is the one that plagues live coverage: Why the rush? The lengthy document was basically a collection of allegations, a de facto indictment based on purported transgressions that had not been proved and that had not yet been presented to the White House for rebuttal. The lurid parts of the report actually constituted a mere sideshow; the substantive charges were not about sex but rather centered on alleged perjury and obstruction of justice. Nevertheless, despite questions about fairness and taste, journalists felt compelled to present the report's contents with few disclaimers other than tantalizing warnings about its graphic content.

One reason for the emphasis on speed was competition from the Internet. As noted in chapter 1, the entire report was available directly on government Web sites and through links from news organizations' sites. Rather than leave the public to its own devices and let people get the news on their own in this way, television news executives decided to try to match the Internet's speed as information provider. The problem with this approach is that merely delivering raw information is not journalism.

The distinction could be seen in newspapers' coverage of the Starr report the following day. Many presented lengthy excerpts and a few, such as the *New York Times*, printed the entire document. But their news stories were carefully considered and structured: emphasis was placed on what was judged most important, caveats were offered about the unproved nature of the allegations, and limits were placed on how much of the sexually graphic material was included.

The Starr report's release was a turning point for the Internet in its relationship with other information media. For many people, the Web was no longer merely an ocean on which to surf for news but had become a primary source. According to

Web traffic tracker RelevantKnowledge, approximately 24.7 million people saw the Starr report during the first two days it was online. That exceeds the circulation of America's fifty largest daily newspapers.[15] Another step forward with the Starr report was improved on-screen format. Software companies are making material easier to read by combining text with a table of contents and scrolling footnotes at the bottom of the screen. The great duel between the computer screen and the printed page centers on convenience for the information consumer. For the Internet site designer, the goal is to minimize the amount of clicking and other maneuvering required to read a document. Graphics should be helpful and not distracting. The trial-and-error approach is quickly moving toward making the Internet a much more reader-friendly medium.

Similar issues of speed, taste, and selectivity arose when the videotapes of Clinton's testimony to Starr's grand jury were released by the House Judiciary Committee. Television hyped the occasion with typically silly excess, putting cameras in the Capitol office where the tapes were delivered and placed in machines to be fed to the networks. The technicians who cued up the tapes may have enjoyed their fleeting moments as national television stars, but this was drama being manufactured out of flimsy material. It illustrated how the desire for a live shot can defeat common sense.

The networks also had to make decisions on the fly about the news value of the testimony as an unedited whole. ABC demonstrated its ambivalence by splitting the screen between the Clinton tape and the president's live speech at the United Nations. The audio, however, was the testimony; the U.N. speech was like a silent movie, but without the helpful captions. ABC's priorities apparently were in line with those of the audience. CNN's Headline News channel carried the U.N. speech but the ratings were low, while CNN's main channel carried the testimony and attracted a large audience.

The big three networks had originally planned to provide only excerpts of the report after it was released, while CNN would offer it whole as soon as it was available. Worried about being upstaged by a cable network, executives at the three principal broadcast networks changed their minds. The combined network audience for this political equivalent of a soap opera was about 22.5 million.[16] Once again, this was information delivery more than real journalism. The testimony was presented without prior reportorial scrutiny, except for reading a transcript that was released at the same time as the tapes. This allowed network news managers to read a little ahead of the video transmission. NBC chose to delete two passages it thought too explicit, and MSNBC deleted one. No one else made any cuts.

Stories anticipating Clinton's testimony had been shaped partly by the unsourced news reports that plagued coverage throughout the scandal. One that had received considerable comment was that Clinton had used profanity and stormed out of the room as he was being questioned. That was simply wrong, and after the fact appeared to have been a setup by Clinton partisans who had wanted to lower expectations about the president's performance. That's clever gamesmanship on the part of Clinton's spin masters, but sloppy journalism on the part of news organizations that let themselves be used. Clinton's standing in opinion polls rose after the testimony aired, in part, presumably, because he had not appeared to lose control as some viewers, relying on news reports, had expected.

The Internet did not seriously challenge television when the testimony tapes were first released because for most computer users the downloading process and video and audio quality do not match the convenience and technical excellence of television. That technological gap certainly will be closed soon, and in the meantime the Net is able to play to its own strengths. For instance, the AltaVista search engine offered the testimony chopped up into pieces and indexed so that Internet users could type in a key word (such as "cigar") and see the portions of the tape containing that word.[17] This capability—like using a book's index—certainly will appeal to news consumers who want some control over the content of news programming. Congressional hearings could be selectively accessed this way, with C-SPAN or other news organizations offering a valuable Web-based research tool. Compare this with the old-fashioned way of finding a quote or other reference in a long document: get the *New York Times* on microfilm and scroll through it until you find what you need. A few strokes on the computer keyboard will replace that.

Building this convenient information retrieval system will take time and will require decisions about priorities. A computerized index of CBS's Vietnam War coverage would be valuable; a Monica Lewinsky concordance, less so. Which will be created first?

WHEN COVERAGE AFFECTS EVENTS

Journalism is not an esoteric enterprise isolated from the rest of society. Even the strongest commitment to detached objectivity does not alter the fact that people react to news. Opinions shift and actions change. Journalists may proclaim while covering a political campaign, for example, that they do not want to affect the outcome of the race. But that makes no sense. Why bother reporting the news if you don't want people to take note of it and act on what they learn? Eliciting such a response should not automatically raise concerns about bias. A straightforward news story might stimulate as much reaction as an editorial does.

Live coverage affects people much the way other journalism does, except the speed of public reaction may match the timeliness of the reporting. The course of events still in progress, as well as their volatility, may be influenced by the kind of coverage they receive. This reinforces the need for accuracy and sophisticated news judgment.

An example of this occurred on April 29, 1992. A Ventura County, California, jury acquitted four Los Angeles police officers being tried for beating Rodney King. The beating had been videotaped and shown throughout the world. It seemed to be a case of such brutal excess that the police officers' conviction was thought to be certain. The jury, however, saw things differently.

Word of the "not guilty" verdict was delivered instantly by television and radio and ignited long-smoldering anger in Los Angeles's African American community. Rioting quickly erupted, which included assaults of nonblacks who happened to be in certain parts of south central Los Angeles. Scattered assaults and looting spread and fires were set. Within a few hours a major riot was under way.

At one particular intersection, Florence and Normandie, a number of assaults took place. They were covered by reporters in helicopters, who also pointed out the absence of police. In his book about the aftermath of the King case, *Official Negligence*, journalist Lou Cannon wrote that "the televised scenes of violence advertised to criminals that the LAPD would not stand in their way and almost certainly fanned the spread of the riots."[18] Ted Koppel, appraising the live television reporting, said, "It is live television at its most riveting and horrifying. But live TV also becomes the carrier of a virus. At one and the same time, television conveys the fever of street violence and the impotence of the police. The beatings, the looting, the arson spread."[19]

Assuming that Cannon and Koppel are correct in their assessments of the effects of the coverage, does that mean that local news organizations were somehow at fault? The rioting was unquestionably newsworthy, and the public had a right and a need to know about it. Nancy Valenta, news director at Los Angeles television station KNBC, later said, "When you're having events happening of that caliber . . . you'd almost be negligent not to go on the air and tell people where there are severe trouble spots." KNBC anchor Jess Marlow added that the coverage did more good than harm because it warned rush-hour commuters and other people away from the riot area.[20]

Sometimes reporters themselves become caught up in events such as this one. KNBC reporter Rick Chambers was doing a live stand-up outside the LAPD's Foothill Division station (where the officers who beat King worked) when he suddenly had to take cover from sniper fire. He kept his on-air composure, later saying that "you try and keep that calm tone and just tell what you see. You know when to turn off lights, when to move and not move. You may inflame the situation when [protestors] feel the media has taken one side."[21]

How reporters handle such situations sends signals to the public about the real state of affairs in the midst of the crisis. They may be hearing calming words from a mayor or police chief, but on-scene journalists provide a more vivid and often more credible appraisal of events. When the reportage is delivered live, thoughtful weighing of words might be set aside. There just isn't time. This raises the stakes. Inaccurate or intemperate words from a journalist can be like matches tossed into a puddle of gasoline. In these situations, journalists' professional responsibility is extraordinarily important.

Live news coverage thrives on exciting stories. When the pace of events sweeps viewers along like a wild flood, the audience is likely to keep watching. Excitement, however, should not be an isolated criterion. Particularly in situations in which the public's safety is involved, journalistic duty should extend beyond rapid delivery of information. Gauging possible reactions to that information becomes part of a news organization's job. Beyond that, commitment to accuracy should intensify to match the intensity of the story at hand.

"SOMETHING MUST BE DONE"

Real-time journalism often delivers the news in easily consumable bites. But these are intellectual snacks, not meals; they satisfy only briefly and leave a hunger for more. There is not enough substance to be truly filling. This issue is not relevant to some news reports, since the story topics themselves—especially spot news items—are shallow and inconsequential. More substantive stories—those that have long-term importance—suffer from high-speed, quick-and-dirty coverage.

So do the audiences that try to make sense of these reports. News does not exist merely to satisfy idle curiosity. Those news consumers who have public policy responsibilities rely on journalism as a source of the information tools they use to build opinion, shape policy, and govern. They know that news coverage can spur the public to demand action about a particular issue. Policy makers are expected to "do something" in response to the version of events presented by the news media. A good example of this can be seen in the relationship between news and policy in foreign affairs.

Real-time news coverage can compress the amount of time governments have for responding to a sudden crisis. The effects of this compression are debatable. One school of thought holds that news coverage—particularly live reporting, with its intrinsic urgency—can drive policy making. But an argument can also be made that the impact of news coverage is overrated and that competent policy makers resist news-generated pressures.

The truth probably falls somewhere in between. Congressman Lee Hamilton, chairman of the House Foreign Affairs Committee, said in 1994:

> Televised images quickly become a central part of the foreign policy debate. They affect which crises we decide to pay attention to and which we ignore. They affect how we think

about these crises, and I have little doubt these televised pictures ultimately affect what we do about these problems.[22]

James Rubin, State Department spokesman while Madeline Albright was secretary of state, said, "The compression of the news cycle has put a greater premium on highly critical reporting." This can keep policy makers on the defensive and, said Rubin, "that harms our ability to get our policy across to the public."[23]

The effects of live news coverage, in foreign affairs as in other subjects, are related to the stories' content. Live reporting—on television, radio, and the Internet—may lack context, detail, and even accuracy, leaving its audience uncertain about how to find the locale in question on a map, much less understand the dynamics of the players and the politics. Nevertheless, such coverage can capture public attention and affect public opinion. Events of recent years provide a number of striking examples of this interplay.

PRIME-TIME WAR

As seen through the television camera's night-vision lens, downtown Baghdad was drenched in a surreal yellow-green glow. For much of the time all was still, the headlights of an automobile occasionally sliding across the screen. Periodically, the night became alive with flashes: small ones dotting the sky, then a larger one—like a torch—moving steadily across the horizon, then a huge burst of light. The shells and bombs crackled and boomed. Reporters gasped and tried to steady their voices. It was quite a show.

This was the scene in mid-December 1998, as the United States and Great Britain launched four days of air strikes against Iraq. Live coverage of combat, such a novelty during the 1991

Gulf War, now was smoothly mixed into the flow of television news.

In this instance, the attack on Iraq provided extra drama as counterpoint to impeachment proceedings against President Bill Clinton that were under way in the U.S. House of Representatives. On Saturday, December 19, as debate proceeded prior to the impeachment vote, the television audience could watch both the House chamber and Baghdad on split screen. It was an impressive, if not particularly meaningful, electronic collage.

For its part, the Clinton administration seemed to have adjusted well to the requisites of prime-time war. White House press secretary Joe Lockhart timed his official announcement about the air strikes to coincide with network television reports from Baghdad about the attack. In a display of military self-confidence, the Pentagon casually let journalists know when a wave of missiles was launched, despite the fact that the audience for CNN and other networks quite likely included members of Saddam Hussein's government.

Hanging over the bombing was a political question: Did President Clinton order the attack as a way to rally public support and impede the impeachment process? Did the White House hope that a dose of "living room war"—engrossing but safely remote violence—would give a final boost to anti-impeachment poll numbers? The administration forcefully denied all such allegations but could not dispel suspicion.

Although it is impossible to determine Clinton's true intent concerning the relationship between the attacks and the impeachment, any president knows that televised images of war—particularly when they are part of real-time coverage—will capture the public's attention and may well stimulate a rally-'round-the-flag response.

As the 1991 Gulf War illustrated, live coverage has complex ramifications for policy makers and journalists. It shrinks time and diminishes flexibility. When the public is seeing events as they happen, policy makers may feel pressed to respond rapidly. When news organizations provide real-time coverage, their journalists must similarly keep pace with the action. Time for reflection—a precious commodity in both government and journalism—may be squeezed to the point of nonexistence. This affects many levels of the news business. By the time of the Gulf War, even local television stations (at least those in major markets) could afford to buy enough satellite time to allow independent live reporting from the war zone.

Despite the censorship imposed by the Bush administration, reporters still found plenty to discuss, but sometimes the quest for drama overwhelmed thoughtful news judgment, and the emphasis on speed superseded fact-checking. Lawrence Grossman, a former president of NBC News, said that television viewers experienced "the illusion of news" because by providing a view of merely the surface of events, "the on-the-scene cameras and live satellite pictures at times served to mask reality rather than shed light on what was happening." He added that "rumors, gossip, speculation, hearsay and unchecked claims were televised live, without verification, without sources, without editing, while we watched newsmen scrambling for gas masks and reacting to missile alerts."[24] Journalist Johanna Neuman wrote that "viewers could not so much see war as they could observe news-gathering in the war zone."[25]

The security problems that can arise from live coverage could be seen when Iraq launched Scud missiles at Israel. The Israeli government was concerned that live television reports about the attack, if seen by the Iraqis, would help them target their missiles. The Israelis quickly agreed with international TV news organizations about guidelines for such coverage. Among the rules were the following:

• An Israeli censor would be in each network's workspace to approve live shots as they were set up and aired.

- If the live location was outdoors, the reporter could be shown only in a tight head shot, with no identifying background visible.
- The number of missiles in an attack and whether they exploded on impact could not be reported unless the information was provided by Israeli authorities.
- No specific locations could be shown; no rising smoke, no wide shots of where the missile hit, no shots that would allow even a general neighborhood to be identified.
- No maps or similar graphics related to the attacked sites could be used.

The last three of these rules applied to taped as well as live reports.

This is censorship, but it is hard to argue against the logic behind it. The Israelis recognized that in circumstances such as those that arose during the Gulf War, television coverage in itself can constitute a significant threat to national security. For their part, most news executives similarly understood that the stakes involved made the Israeli guidelines reasonable. Live reporting from the site targeted by a missile or artillery attack can cast reporters in the role of spotters for the attackers. In the Gulf War, the Iraqi high command was known to watch CNN and other international news broadcasters. If they saw, for example, a live news report with smoke rising from a point on the Tel Aviv skyline, they would know if their attack had been on target and, if not, what adjustments to make before the next missile launch.

Government can sometimes wield considerable influence in shaping coverage of its actions. What it cannot afford, however, is to underestimate the potential impact of live reporting about a war or similar foreign policy event. For both journalism and government, speed is important. Policy makers will find themselves at a political disadvantage if their efforts lag too far behind the pace set by news coverage. The Persian Gulf War was brief—the ground war lasting only about 100 hours. But as the first war to be covered live, it provided some valuable lessons for coverage of future conflicts:

- Security and censorship. Governments can make an irrefutable argument about the need to control live reporting that may be seen by the enemy (as virtually all satellite broadcasting can be). Real-time information about deployment of forces or after-action status is priceless intelligence and indiscriminate dissemination simply cannot be allowed. News organizations should recognize this and design their own guidelines that balance reporting duties with security realities. A self-imposed embargo for a reasonable time would take care of much of this problem. There is no reason journalists cannot do this for themselves, rather than wait for government officials to impose their own rules. If news organizations take the initiative on this, they may be in a better position to resist other censorship that is motivated more by political than by security concerns.
- Combat and casualties. Since the Gulf War, the truck-carried flyaway transmitter has shrunk, making it even more mobile and allowing even more opportunities for real-time reporting. Live coverage of combat is technologically easier, and it would unquestionably be audience grabbing. But this is real fighting, not a movie; these are real soldiers, not actors; and this is real blood, not Hollywood makeup. News organizations should consider the impact such coverage would have, especially on the families of the combatants, and even more particularly on the families of those who are killed or wounded. "News," regardless of its accuracy and impact, should not be allowed to override basic decency.
- Delivering news and delivering messages. Live coverage

carries information not only from journalists to their mass audience but also from government to government. Going on CNN is faster than using the diplomatic pouch. This kind of public diplomacy may, however, comprise both substance and propaganda; governments have been known to be less than truthful, particularly during wars and other crises. When a lie is delivered by journalists, it is delivered as news, perhaps lending it more credibility than it deserves. News organizations may want to be helpful by providing electronic courier service, but they should be alert to being manipulated.

There is nothing particularly hard to understand about these matters. The task for news professionals is simply to recognize the many facets and ramifications of live coverage during wartime, anticipate as many contingencies as possible, and design some general operating principles that can be used when making coverage decisions at such times.

News coverage is likely to have most effect on a weak policy-making process. A firm, principled policy foundation probably will not be shaken by news reports and resultant public demands that "something must be done!" Peter Jennings of ABC News observed that "political leadership trumps good television every time. As influential as television can be, it is most influential in the absence of decisive political leadership."[26] Nevertheless, policy makers should brace themselves for a surge of emotion-driven public opinion in the wake of graphic news coverage of events such as war or famine. This is especially true when the coverage is live, since these reports carry an additional drama of their own. Professor Steven Livingston, who studies media and foreign policy, has noted that "the creation of global real-time television has undermined the diplomat's ability to mediate between distant events and the public."[27] Policy makers also should keep in mind that journalists are not infallible and that their reports—no matter how well supported with convincing video—sometimes may be incomplete, may lack nuance, or may simply be wrong.

For their part, news organizations should be sensitive to governments' relying on their coverage when it serves as messenger, early warning system, and general gatherer of information about goings-on elsewhere. The traditional prerogatives of the diplomat have been usurped to some extent by this expanded news media capability. The erosion will continue as communications technology becomes more sophisticated. Private spy satellites and Internet communication are among the tools journalists will use to acquire and disseminate the kinds of information that once remained exclusively within governments' domain. Steven Livingston has said that not only will policies be measured against what is seen on television, but they also will be "constantly measured against a more comprehensive array of information and images—including satellite images—found on television and on the Web." This reliance should lead to a renewed commitment to thoroughness and accuracy on the part of those who deliver the news.

As a corollary to this, journalists who present live reports should beware of being manipulated by those who want to affect policy via the news media. With so much emphasis on speed, the temptation may arise to shortchange corroboration of sources and other fact-checking procedures. Suspending disbelief inevitably leads to errors.

The Internet will be an increasingly significant factor in foreign policy and its coverage. Of particular importance will be the ability of interest groups to deliver their messages to wider audiences. During humanitarian crises, for example, relief agencies will use their Web sites to make the case for assistance. How public opinion and governmental response are affected by this will vary from case to case. Much will depend on whether news organizations avail themselves of the opportunity to use these sites as information sources.

Part of the egalitarian power of the Internet lies in its ability to be accessed directly by the public, regardless of how the news media respond. But mere availability of information means little in itself. The public has to find it, care about it, and act upon it before it really matters. Information, absent such a response, is worth very little. It is reasonable to hope, however, that when online news sites devote even terse reports about famine, refugee crises, or other such matters, they will include links to public and private agencies' Web sites so news consumers who care, however small their numbers, can get additional information and perhaps become involved. Humanitarian relief organizations will use e-mail to alert their constituencies and raise money. By expanding awareness about a situation, they might push news organizations to provide more thorough coverage. That may make a difference.

More generally, the Internet should help break down barriers that obstruct the cross-national flow of information. During the 1989 Tiananmen Square crisis, the Chinese government was able to block or otherwise manipulate incoming television coverage. That will be much harder to do when coverage is moving through the World Wide Web. Before long, no country and no people will be beyond the Internet's reach. News organizations, governments, and their publics will have to decide what to do with this vast new reservoir of information.

As this media expansion takes place, a general conclusion about the effect of real-time coverage on foreign policy will probably remain constant. The accumulated case evidence is that this kind of reporting has been and will continue to be influential but not determinative in its effect on policy. That distinction is important.

Just as the Vietnam War was the living room war and the Gulf War was the first live war, the 1999 war in Kosovo was the first Web war. This conflict illustrated the impact of the Internet on the news media's reporting. Although mainstream news organizations used their own Web sites, the Internet dramatically changed journalists' gatekeeper role. Web users could create their own array of sources, moving with a click of the mouse from the White House to the Serbian Ministry of Information, taking and believing whatever they wanted from each. This was a good example of unmediated media: no filter, no editorial judgments, no commentary or context beyond what was offered on the screen by the unchallenged source.

Some news consumers may have found the intellectual freedom they had long wanted: "No network anchor is telling us what to think; no editor is chopping out paragraphs that we might find interesting. We can gather news just as journalists do and decide for ourselves what to make of it." Yet with limited ability to verify information picked up at various Web sites, independent news gatherers are at the mercy of their sources.

News organizations facilitated this independence by providing links from their own Web sites. CNN, for example, offered a long list of war-related links, such as ones to the Kosovo Liberation Peace Movement, the Central Intelligence Agency's *World Factbook* (for CIA-compiled information about Serbia and Montenegro), a freelance journalist's site with a road map of Kosovo, refugee assistance agencies, and a number of audio and video offerings. Individuals trapped in the battle zone sent their own e-mail messages to the world. On its site, Radio Yugoslavia denounced NATO as "the fascists of the new world order," and NATO on its site offered video sequences of its recent air strikes. For the news consumer, this marriage of smart bomb and home computer was a new kind of journalism—a self-produced mix of high-tech war movie and newscast.

CNN's list of Web connections was preceded by a parenthetical note stating, "These sites are not endorsed by CNN Interactive." But Web users moving from the principal CNN site to the links it offered may have had no real sense of leaving the news organization's premises. News seekers moving among cybersources may have met the shrill pronouncements of some sites with skepticism but may have accepted subtle spin as fact.

When the line between news and information blurs in this way, journalists and policy makers should take note. The public's attitude toward traditional news media may be affected by whatever it finds on the fringes of the Web. "Dan Rather is telling me about this story, but I know I saw exactly the opposite somewhere on the Web." Similarly, government officials explaining policy will have to compete with dissonant voices using the Internet as electronic soapbox. The Web will educate with unpredictable effect.

In response to the ever growing flow of Web-based information, news organizations might decide to emphasize their role as providers of context and analysis. At some point, even the most independent Web surfers may want a little help. Making sense of the world is not necessarily easier just because more information is available.

Online news coverage of the world will keep expanding. The "CNN effect" has become old hat. The Web has overtaken all-news television because of the almost infinite variety of sites and links it can feature.

Journalists will try to find their place in all this. As the war in the Balkans showed, the amount of easily available news grows steadily. Somewhere in the midst of all that news is truth. Journalists still have a role in finding it.

3

FROM BROADCAST TO CABLE TO WEB

The twentieth century was the era of radio and television. Commercial radio took hold in the 1920s. Communications scholar Susan J. Douglas has written:

> Radio is arguably the most important electronic invention of the century. Cognitively, it revolutionized the perceptual habits of the nation. Technically, culturally, and economically, it set the stage for television. It forever blurred the boundaries between the private domestic sphere and public, commercial, and political life.[1]

Douglas notes, however, that radio today is "low-tech, unglamorous, and taken for granted." During the 1950s, the TV set became an integral part of the American household. It soon became the public's dominant daily news source, overshadowing radio and print. Until the late 1990s, television seemed well entrenched as a communication tool of the same magnitude as the printing press. Its journalistic functions may have been criticized as being more showy than substantive, but its influence was undisputed.

Radio, meanwhile, had enjoyed a resurgence on two levels. Although its audience was relatively small, National Public Radio established itself as one of the country's most thoughtful and thorough news sources. On a far larger scale, but far less thoughtful and thorough, was the rejuvenated talk radio. Local talk shows proliferated, and nationally Rush Limbaugh led an array of provocative talkers who flaunted their biases and attracted huge followings.

Television was especially susceptible, for technological reasons, to sweeping change. The arrival of widespread cable access ended the near-monopoly of the big three broadcast networks: ABC, CBS, and NBC. CNN proved that there is a market for all-news television, and during the 1991 Gulf War it established itself as a viable rival to the broadcast networks' news divisions. Viewers who once had to choose among a handful of channels now had fifty or more, with promises of additional hundreds on the way from cable or satellite providers. Two-thirds of television viewers subscribe to cable, and in 1998 cable viewing for the first time exceeded the broadcast networks' combined audience.[2] In its intensifying competition with cable, the direct broadcast satellite business claimed 10 million subscribers in early 2000.

Most of cable television is controlled by a few giants, such as Time Warner and AT&T. This dominance can pose a threat to viewers, as illustrated in May 2000, when a battle between Time Warner and Disney, which owns ABC, resulted in Time Warner temporarily dropping ABC from its offerings in several cities, affecting more than 3 million viewers.

In recent years, the big three networks have seen their slice of the audience pie grow steadily smaller and their revenues shrink accordingly. Viewers sampled alternative fare, either on cable channels or on new networks such as Fox, Warner Bros., and Paramount. In 1997, only 41 percent of Americans said they watched a nightly network news program regularly, down from 60 percent in 1993.[3] Regardless of whether the wandering viewer was watching another news program or something like the Golf Channel, the hegemony of the established order was over.

Sometimes the big three yield ground willingly. On December 11, 1998, when the House Judiciary Committee completed its debate and voted on articles of impeachment against President Bill Clinton, ABC, CBS, and NBC carried only the actual vote, leaving coverage of the committee's debate to CNN, MSNBC, Fox News, C-SPAN, and some PBS stations. Executives at the major networks said the public interest was being served adequately by the cable channels. Some added that they thought the public was not interested in seeing a predictable debate about a topic that most people were tired of. As a journalistic decision, this may have been questionable, but the appraisal of the audience was apparently correct. The combined audience for CNN, MSNBC, and Fox News was slightly less than 2 million viewers, considerably larger than their normal audience but far smaller than the number that CNN alone had attracted to its coverage of the O.J. Simpson trial.[4]

In April 2000, when six-year-old Cuban Elian Gonzalez was taken by federal authorities from his relatives' home in Miami, CNN, MSNBC, and Fox News Channel carried extensive coverage and attracted much larger than normal audiences. These networks are developing a constituency of news viewers who turn to them as the most likely source of uninterrupted coverage of stories such as this one.

This shift in coverage prerogative reflects a significant change in how television news organizations view their professional responsibilities. During the 1960s, for example, the networks (especially CBS and NBC) competed fiercely to be identified as the public's principal broadcast news source. In 1966, CBS News president Fred Friendly became embroiled in a bitter dispute with his network's top executives when they refused his request to carry live, weekday morning coverage of Senate hearings about the Vietnam War, choosing instead to air reruns of *I Love Lucy* and *The Real McCoys*. Friendly saw this as such an irresponsible decision that he resigned from the network. At the time, there was no CNN or C-SPAN alternative. The role of the big three networks as gatekeepers was taken for granted, and a decision such as the one by CBS not to carry the hearings was certain to be controversial. Today, the major networks' commitment to news has changed, and deferring to the cable news channels on a major story barely gets noticed.

Digital technology, which compresses the television signal so that it can carry more information, promises still greater expansion of television offerings. The viewer may be able to choose from among more than a thousand channels that will provide niche programming targeted at niche audiences. This programming will be far more sophisticated than traditional TV fare. It will have interactive features that today are usually associated with the Internet, not television. Basketball fans will probably have the National Basketball Association Channel. They will be able to decide how they want to watch the game, selecting overhead, sideline, or behind-the-basket camera shots as they please. Virtually every hobby and business field will have its own programming.

Where the profits will come from is still uncertain, and no one can predict how audiences will change their viewing habits. But television executives assume that consumers, once they see the huge array of new televised options, will pay a premium to hook up to digital service and then pick and choose a substantial number of favorite channels. Advertisers may similarly pay a premium to reach audiences that have divided themselves into special interest clusters. Robert Decherd, president, chairman, and CEO of A. H. Belo Corporation, cites "digital localism" as a new strategy: using digital capabilities and ownership of various media properties in a community to create new revenue streams while offering diverse news and entertainment products.[5]

The presence of digital technology will be a momentous change in the way television is used. Tom Tyrer, Fox Broadcasting's vice president of corporate communications, said: "People sometimes say this is like the transition from black-and-white to color television. It's not. It's like the transition from radio to television. It's a whole new world."⁶

TELEVISION'S WEB

As mandated by the Federal Communications Commission, television will have converted from analog to digital service by 2006. Despite the intriguing appeal of digital capability, however, television news organizations are looking beyond traditional television mechanisms as the means of delivering their product. Cautiously but steadily, they are adopting the Internet as a supplemental medium.

The logic behind this effort is simple: go where the audience is. With the explosive growth in the number of Internet users, news organizations simply cannot stay off the Web. Although early data offer conflicting verdicts about Internet versus television use, there is sufficient basis to fear losing at least some television watchers some of the time to online pursuits. Rather than have to play catch-up if a pronounced trend away from television develops, the TV news industry is establishing a significant presence on the Net.

This presence exists on two levels. The first is at the portal, the major Web site that is the user's point of entry onto the Internet. Yahoo, for example, reports tens of millions of visitors each month. On the "front page" of the portal is a list of news headlines, ready for a quick scan. Anyone who wants more details simply clicks and a list of specific stories appears. Clicking on an international story headline calls up a list of stories that may include items from Reuters, Arabic News, CNN, and Associated Press. Also available are video clips from ABC, BBC, and others.

A survey conducted in late 1998 for media research firm Jupiter Communications found that the majority of online news consumers wanted headlines and summaries, so Jupiter recommended that online news providers "develop content around major and breaking stories rather than produce deep analysis." This approach is appealing because it is relatively easy to assemble headlines and keep them updated. Particularly when a major breaking story dominates the news, many Internet users may want to check the status of the story periodically. Terse, up-to-the-minute summaries may suffice. Some news sites offer a continuing stream of headlines across the bottom of the computer screen and send e-mail to users with updates about stories concerning topics that the user has selected.

The portal owner is not a truly neutral provider of information. Whether it is Yahoo, America Online/Netscape, or even a rarely visited site owner, someone must make editorial judgments about what headlines to feature—what is newsworthy. On a Web site, as on a newspaper or newscast, that decision-making role carries with it significant power. News consumers are being told that these are the stories meriting headlines and their attention. If the "editor" of a site decided, for example, in 1998 to make that site "all Monica, all the time," its audience would be shortchanged in coverage of other news (and there was other news) besides the White House scandal. The site visitors could, of course, go elsewhere, either instead of or in addition to the "all Monica" site. How many sources Internet news consumers will seek out is as yet unknown. There will be some clicking from site to site (much like clicking between channels with a TV remote control), but most users are likely to rely on a relatively small number of favorite sites.

Another power, at least as important as headline selection, in the hands of portal editors is the choice of links. When site visitors click on links, they might not pay much attention to where they are being taken, instead trusting the portal provider's judgment about this. If portal-based news delivery is to be considered a serious journalistic function, then accuracy and balance in linked news sources is crucial.

Yet the headlines and limited additional information that portals offer may not be enough to satisfy the news consumer. As opposed to the delivery-at-the-portal approach, news organizations will develop their own Web sites as providers of supplemental information. This is particularly true for television news, which has long been criticized as lacking the substance of print news providers.

Properly developed, a Web site can do much to rebut such criticism. The background information and contextual depth that have been mainly the domain of print news organizations now are available from television sources on the Web. In January 1999, as President Clinton's impeachment trial began, ABC News provided live coverage during part of the day as well as newscast summaries of the day's events. But the network's Web site offered a massive amount of information:

- articles of impeachment
- trial rules
- profiles of the House prosecution team and the chief justice
- description of the 1868 impeachment trial of Andrew Johnson
- the Starr report and additional materials, plus the White House rebuttal
- a timeline beginning in early 1998, with still more links
- video clips of Clinton's grand jury testimony, indexed by topic

With these and many more items accessible at the click of a mouse, the ABC site would presumably satisfy most impeachment aficionados. Such treasuries of information allow television news organizations to assume a role that traditionally has

belonged to the *New York Times* and scholarly publications—
repository of record—the source to which news junkies and researchers can turn for the primary materials of history. There is
no reason that a television network's Web site cannot offer as
thorough an array of background material as the *New York Times*
can. This is another example of Internet as equalizer.

Not every story lends itself to the exhaustive treatment that
the Clinton impeachment received, but as time passes Web site
users will become accustomed to finding at least some background material about every major story. While the Clinton trial
was getting under way, another important story concerned military action in Iraq. The CBS News Web site provided a report
about an American aircraft firing on an Iraqi surface-to-air missile site. This story was offered in text form with an audio report
from a correspondent in Turkey, plus a map of the no-fly zone
and a link to the U.S. European Command. This site offered the
Defense Department's official announcement about the attack,
the formal definition of the no-fly zone restrictions, and even
further links with information about the F-16, the U.S. aircraft
that was involved in the incident.

With stories such as this, the link-to-link path becomes almost endless, leading far beyond what the news organization itself provides. A major question about this process concerns the
extent to which CBS News, in this case, is vouching for the material provided by the Pentagon. The news consumer originally
came to CBS for information and got the basic story on the network's site. But does that news consumer recognize that with a
click of the mouse he or she has moved into nonjournalistic terrain? The information from the Department of Defense probably
does not provide the balance that would be expected of a journalistic account. How far does the news organization's responsibility extend in terms of verifying and vouching for the accuracy
of the information from the linked source?

Accuracy and balance are both concerns. In the story cited

above about the military confrontation between the United States and Iraq, suppose an organization called "Justice for Iraq" has a Web site that purveys propaganda provided by Saddam Hussein's government, the accuracy of which is dubious. Should CBS provide a link to this site? If so, should a disclaimer be appended that notes the site's connection to the Iraqi government? If that is done, should a similar disclaimer be added to the links from the same story to U.S. government sites?

Standard journalistic practice does not usually give interested parties such unfiltered access to the public. Journalists screen material from sources, checking its accuracy as well as they can, and then use it, if they choose to do so, as part of a balanced story. Before the imprimatur of an organization such as CBS News goes on a story, the material has, presumably, been through this process. Some critics of the news media, however, argue that this is precisely what is wrong with journalism—that this screening and selectivity is influenced by various biases and therefore the news is distorted before it reaches the public. Based on this argument, the news organization's Internet product should provide as many links as possible and let news consumers decide what they want to believe and what they choose to ignore.

That laissez-faire approach becomes problematic when the linked site provides information that is wrong and perhaps malicious. As a matter of free speech, constrained by libel and slander law, the originator of that site should be able to say whatever he or she wants, but that does not necessarily mean that CBS or any other news organization should implicitly sponsor its dissemination through a link from its own site.

These issues are not limited to television news organizations but apply to any Web site that provides news. At present, the Web sites of television and radio news networks and stations are most committed to live coverage of breaking news. But that will certainly change as print news organizations expand their

Web presence and technological capabilities. Just as verifying source material for stories delivered by conventional means is accepted as a principal journalistic responsibility, so will vetting linked sources be part of the evolving ethics of online journalism.

In online newsrooms, decisions about these matters may have to be made quickly. MSNBC, a joint venture between Microsoft and NBC that made its debut in 1996, offers on-air and online products. For the latter, producers assemble multimedia components that include material from NBC and non–broadcast news sources with which it has agreements, such as the *Washington Post*. It provides links to MSNBC's cable incarnation and to NBC products such as *The Today Show*. The site also runs altogether new or at least expanded versions of stories that can find a home on the Web site even when squeezed out of broadcast rundowns.

Many international stories are particularly well suited to online news because of the global audience that visits the Web site. Worldwide access and the resulting change in the audience may reshape the conventional wisdom about what stories will attract viewers and readers. The provincialism of American news consumers has fostered a decline in international news coverage by major news organizations (especially television). In many other countries, however, interest in the rest of the world is higher. That might lead American news organizations to rethink their priorities and expand their foreign coverage.

MSNBC's audience is growing. According to *PC Data Online*, it was reaching an average of 2.7 million unique visits weekly by early 2000, making it the most visited news Web site. (The "unique visitors" figure represents the number of users who visited the site once during the week of the survey. Multiple visits were not counted.) There have been occasional surges, such as on the day the Starr report was released, when the site had 2 million visitors.[7] Merrill Brown, editor in chief of MSNBC on the Internet, has said, "We are constantly trying to figure out how to tell the story, how to integrate multimedia, how to use computer software to tell the story, and striving to operate at some level in sync with our cable counterpart." This is new territory for journalists. "This is like television in 1947," said Brown.[8]

Adventurous journalists like the challenges they find in exploring this terrain. Sheila Kaplan, who had been a newspaper reporter and a producer for ABC, took a job as a producer with MSNBC, saying, "To me MSNBC was the best of both worlds: taking the substance of print and adding in the creativity of TV, without having the constraints of length and space."[9] Kari Huus, a former print and radio reporter who became a foreign correspondent for MSNBC, told about covering a breaking story during the 1998 turmoil in Indonesia:

> Had I been a newspaper or magazine reporter, I would have been taking notes and planning to go back to the hotel to write only when my weekly or daily print deadline was upon me. Had I been working in television or radio, I would have been shooting with a particular news slot in mind. But writing for the Internet, making the usual editorial calls— when and how much to file—is more complicated. The medium's strongest suits—speed and versatility—mean that the scope of choices is enormous.[10]

Among her options was recording sound and taking still digital photographs and e-mailing them to MSNBC editors for immediate use. Or she could have used a digital video camera and sent those images through phone lines for instant airing on the MSNBC site. In addition to her real-time coverage, Huus worked on background pieces such as an interactive outline of Indonesia's political leadership. A visitor to the MSNBC Web site could click on a photo of a member of President Suharto's family and see a summary of any controversy about that person's business dealings. This variety of forms of news presentation, wrote Huus, helps make Internet reporting "rich and timely." She noted, however, that the science of providing news this way remains an uncertain one: "the results can also be confusing, incomplete or overwhelming."[11]

Networks may develop hybrids such as MSNBC as their Web offerings in order to establish related but separate identities as news providers. Even when content on the air and on the Web are virtually the same about any given story, other considerations demand separation.

Advertising is one big reason for this. As advertising on the Internet becomes more sophisticated and more profitable, Web-specific strategies for producing ad dollars will become a dominant concern of this segment of the news business. The relationship between ABC News and abcnews.com, for example, will be one featuring not only cooperation but also competition, if not initially in news gathering then certainly in revenue gathering.

Setting standards for news site advertising will require consideration of issues such as these:

- Delineation between news and advertising material. The television audience generally understands the commercial break. The 60–120 seconds consumed at various intervals in a newscast are recognized as selling, not reporting. The graphics of a Web site, however, do not necessarily make that same clean break between news product and ad product. The icon leading to an advertiser's link may strongly resemble one leading to a news link. Making certain that there is clear separation between news and ad content may be a good idea. The amount of advertising on the page/screen at any time is also an issue. Ad messages can visually overwhelm news content.
- The potential for conflicts of interest. The relationship of advertising to actual sales transactions can be tracked much more precisely on a Web site than through television. The ad directed at a television viewer is trying to

stimulate future action, but the Web ad may try to elicit an immediate response—a purchase or at least an inquiry made directly from the site. That encourages a direct percentage payoff to the site's owner, in addition to a general ad fee. Suppose, for example, General Motors advertises on the CBS News site. It pays a fee based on the number of visitors the site has, similar to fees based on television ratings. CBS may charge a supplemental fee based on the number of hits the ad link receives. That could create a conflict of interest more severe than the one that threatens the traditional television news organization–advertiser relationship, perhaps enticing CBS to avoid negative stories about GM. Most journalists would recoil from such a prospect, but network bean counters might have a less rigorous standard of propriety.

- Internet technology itself may create business-related pressures that journalists should note. MSNBC's Kari Huus wrote that "there are definitely things that worry me as a journalist. On the Internet, readership can be tracked better than any other medium—down to how many readers visit a given page and for how long. Marketing people love this, but for journalists the risk of writing market-driven stories instead of important stories has never been greater."[12]
- Gimmickry may become ubiquitous. In 1999, MSNBC offered its site visitors a daily lottery: once the consumer registered for the contest, every visit became an entry in a giveaway of Continental Airlines frequent-flyer miles. Harmless, perhaps, but also more clutter and further coziness between a news organization and an advertiser.
- Ties among the owners of Internet news service. Interlocking ownership can be a problem in all areas of journalism, but it may be particularly severe for online news providers because of how newsworthy many Web-related issues are.

Some of the conflicts are obvious: will news consumers question the integrity of MSNBC stories about Microsoft?

A 1998 survey conducted by Jupiter Communications found that nearly 70 percent of online news consumers said they were not worried about the objectivity of news providers that also sell goods online.[13] But looking at the figures another way reveals that almost a third of this audience may have concerns about this. That is a substantial number, and it should lead to careful examination of the news-commerce linkage on news Web sites.

News organizations will inch their way along as they define the standards that will govern their new media products. Traditional principles will remain valid, but their application to new forms of news delivery will require refinement. To be effective, ethical standards should be both solid and flexible, a combination that is difficult—but essential—to sustain.

LOCAL NEWS ON THE WEB

Television journalism is divided into two fundamental parts: network and local news organizations. Although some of their number are frequently criticized for providing little more than substance-free sensationalism, local newscasts remain America's most popular source of news (see table 3.1).

Table 3.1   News Sources

	Regularly	*Sometimes*
Watch network TV news	41	31
Watch local TV news	72	16
Watch CNN	28	30
Read a daily newspaper	56	24

Source: 1997 study by the Pew Research Center for the People and the Press.

This level of allegiance is not surprising. After all, the local newscast delivers information that most directly affects its audience: the approach of severe weather, a crisis in the local schools, hometown football scores. Perhaps these matters are not as consequential as global warming and Middle East peace, but they are far less abstract to most viewers. Enhancing the appeal of local news organizations is the assiduous promotion of their product as a community asset, delivered by journalists who are marketed as civic celebrities.

But all is not well in the relationship between local television and its viewers. A study released in 2000 by Insite Media Research found substantial viewer dissatisfaction, with a growing number of people avoiding local TV news or, when they watch, not caring which station they watch. Unhappy survey respondents cited repetition in the stories being covered and too much sensationalism and "bad news" as reasons for their disaffection.

With shaky viewer support, local television news organizations, like the networks, see the Internet as a way to improve their product and expand their audience. Although lacking the vast resources of an MSNBC, local stations can build sites that play to their own strengths, including their network affiliation. The CBS Network on the Web, for example, which was launched in 1998, links local CBS affiliates to the network's site. Participating affiliates' Web sites feature the CBS brand name and a mix of network-provided national and international news and affiliate-generated local reports.

This packaging can be used easily by the affiliate—too easily, according to some critics. They argue that local stations should not let their own identities be overshadowed by the network and that a good local product—emphasizing issues important to the community—should be the dominant presence on the site.[14] For one thing, the smartest approach to making money from the site may be having a vehicle that the local audience and local advertisers will find appealing. KLAS, the CBS affiliate in Las Vegas, Nevada, offers CBS reports as part of its online news package, as well as a yellow pages directory and a real estate guide.[15] Baltimore's WJZ features classified ads from a California company specializing in online classified advertising that is sorted by geographic region. Other local stations are also adding features: entertainment listings, restaurant guides, event calendars, and other devices designed to appeal to casual news consumers.

In a similar vein, radio stations are promoting their on-air stars and the contests that they run on their broadcasts. Radio on the Web had an early edge on TV sites because Web technology has allowed live audio feeds to be much cleaner than most video.

In addition, the Web expands potential radio and TV audiences from local to worldwide, and local media are trying to take advantage of at least parts of this vastly expanded market. In 2000, some radio stations began advertising on billboards outside the area that their over-the-air signal would reach, targeting prospective online listeners.

Besides receiving assistance from a network, local stations can select from among a growing number of Internet entrepreneurs whose specialty is building stations' presence on the Web. Among them is International Broadcasting Systems, which contracts with stations to establish and run their Web sites. One of their clients is Minneapolis's WCCO, for which IBS created Channel 4000. The site's staff works in the WCCO newsroom, but the editorial and sales personnel are employed by IBS, not the station itself.[16] Channel 4000 won the National Press Club's Online Journalism Award for its coverage in 1997 (the site's first year of operation) of severe floods in Minnesota and North Dakota. A Web site can handle that kind of story very effectively, providing constantly updated reports about a topic that is truly important but not quite important enough for the television station to blow out its regular programming for all-day live news coverage.

Even on a regular basis, when no big story is being reported, the local Web site has its niche. According to IBS marketing director Andrea Yoc, "If people want national news, they go to CNN.com or ABCnews.com. If they want to find out about traffic, they come to us."[17] Reid Johnson, also with IBS, underscored the importance of this local focus: "In every communications revolution, the local information play has been the most important. . . . The question is, who's going to do it? The newspapers? The broadcasters? Or some independent entity?"[18]

On the business side, IBS noted that it "drives 'convergence' viewers and revenue dollars back to the TV stations. . . . Several of our current broadcast partners have achieved significant ratings gains, and credit their highly trafficked, co-branded Web site for a healthy portion of their success." IBS cited the example that in the Minneapolis area, 39 percent of Channel 4000 users reported that they saw something on the Web site that drew them to watch WCCO, the TV partner, and 49 percent had seen something on WCCO that led them to check the co-branded Channel 4000 site.[19]

By early 2000, the great majority of local TV stations in the United States had Web sites. This trailed the newspaper industry's commitment to the Web, presumably for several reasons. Newspapers took early notice of Internet competitors' potential for seizing part of the classified advertising market. Also, Web sites were better suited to text than to video content, given the effect of bandwidth limitations on video streaming. This problem is diminishing as Web technology improves, making the Internet much more hospitable to television providers and stimulating a surge in the number of Web sites maintained by local stations.

Among other things, this will mean a new level of intensity in the competition between television and newspapers. David Noack, associate editor of *Editor and Publisher Interactive*, wrote, "The franchise that newspapers have long held—in-depth and comprehensive coverage of an issue or event—is giving way in this new medium, where there is a bottomless newshole and innovative ways to present the news."[20] Along the same lines, Jason Primus of IBS said, "We are using the strength of our Web medium to dig deeper on many stories in ways that television and radio stations never could. On the other hand, we are jumping far ahead of local print outlets by posting live updated information throughout the day."[21] The Web staff accomplishes this by monitoring satellite feeds from the station's remote camera trucks. Even if the station does not use that feed immediately, saving the video for a later newscast, the Web site might use it earlier, either in real time as it is received or after a brief delay.[22]

As with conventional live television reporting, real-time coverage through the Web site has an allure that can lead to problems. Taking the remote feed from the station's satellite truck and sending it on to Web watchers is expeditious delivery, but is it journalism? In the control room of a television station, the producer and director can look at a bank of screens and see what the station's cameras and other sources (such as network feeds) are offering. They then select the images that become part of the on-air product. For any reason—technical or editorial—they may decide to withhold, temporarily or permanently, some of those images. That exercise of judgment may be neglected if there is a predisposition to stream raw footage on the Web site without similar oversight. As a systemic matter, the content of a television news organization's Web site should not be exempt from careful editorial evaluation, either by the Web staff members themselves (assuming they have journalistic as well as technical expertise) or by the sponsoring news organization's managers.

Beyond live coverage, Web technology allows television news to offer a product that promises to have considerable audience appeal. WRAL Television in Raleigh, North Carolina, is among the stations with high-quality sites (WRAL.com). It offers live video streaming of its newscasts, which is useful to the viewer sitting at a computer terminal who lacks access to a television set. That service matches what the television viewer gets. But WRAL on the Web also makes its newscasts available from their archives. This is one of the Web's dominating advantages: consumers can decide for themselves when they want to watch the news. More and more stations are doing this as the public begins to prefer having "news on demand" instead of depending on networks' and stations' schedules.

WRAL also offers an interesting gimmick to its Web visitors: a choice of live shots from the newsroom and several area locations (including Animal Cam, showing pets up for adoption at a local shelter). Often nothing is happening at these sites, but the premise is intriguing. The viewer calls up the camera shot he or she wants to see.

Combined with updating of stories, this variety can make the Web site a turn-to source of information that, even in its early stages, foreshadows a cultural change. By the 1960s, television had superseded radio to become the primary source for information about what is happening *now*. With the Internet poised to push aside television and assume that role, television news organizations are beginning to confront a new reality: either move apace with this revolution or be left behind with a smaller and less profitable piece of the information delivery business.

In Toronto, Canada, channel CablePulse 24 demonstrates how the look of television might change. It presents seven fields of information on-screen simultaneously: traditional video, headlines, sports scores, current stock prices or—when the markets are closed—an entertainment calendar, weather conditions, live shots selected from 139 traffic cameras on Toronto-area highways, and ads. The station's general manager, Stephen Hurlbut, said, "We want to blur the line between the news channel and the Web site." The format proved successful. At its start in 1998, the channel attracted 800,000 viewers each week. By late 1999, the weekly audience had grown to 2.2 million.[23]

This is a step toward a more sophisticated marriage between TV and Web. Part of television's adjustment to this relationship may be made easier by a merging of TV and Internet hardware. Instead of viewing both a television and a computer screen, the consumer will have access to both at once. ABC News, for example, will present its evening newscast complete with a Web site menu on the screen. After watching a two-minute story about conflict in the Middle East, the viewer wants to know more. Using a remote control clicker, he or she selects "Background" from the menu along the side of the screen. That produces yet another list, including text, graphics, and video selections. The viewer can pull up an interactive map of the region, point to Damascus or Jerusalem or Cairo or wherever and get still more choices about historical or current events there. The viewer who wants still more might call up a gallery of photos of the major players in the region's politics and access background information, including text or video/audio of recent speeches. The range of options is huge, and they all are coming from the screen. Whether the screen is part of a television or a computer will become an irrelevant distinction. This is convergence.

As the marriage between traditional news organizations and the Internet becomes more established, news consumers are accepting the online product. A survey in late 1998 found that 80 percent of online consumers in the United States trust Internet-delivered news as much as they trust broadcast and cable news outlets and newspapers. Seven percent of the respondents even reported that they consider online news sources *more* reliable than their traditional counterparts.[24] Reasons for this trust may be rooted in the sheer volume of material that Internet sites provide. The apparent absence of editorial discrimination may be reassuring to those who perceive bias in the selection of the product that traditional news vehicles provide. Of course, lack of filtering brings with it other problems, principally the danger of inaccuracies infecting news content. News consumers' priorities about these matters will become better defined as time passes and Internet news becomes more a staple than a novelty.

MORE THAN A DELIVERY SYSTEM

The Internet will allow television news organizations to do more than simply offer their product in a different form. It can also build new bridges between journalists and the public they serve.

A frequently heard complaint about television news is that it is one-way communication that does not take feedback from the audience. Most television news programs lack the equivalent of a newspaper's letters to the editor column. Also, corrections, if made at all, tend to be presented so haphazardly that they might not offset any damage done by the error that is being corrected. The excuse most often offered by television news managers is that their crowded format does not allow such features.

Isolation impairs accountability. A Web site, however, opens the door for easy contact between the public and TV news organizations. A letters to the executive producer page can post e-mail messages from viewers and responses from the station or network. The site can also provide links to individual reporters' e-mail boxes. When corrections to stories are appropriate, they can be made both on the air and on the Web site, which will increase the chances that they will be noticed. The December 1998 Pew study found that 41 percent of respondents thought it was very or fairly important that Web sites allowed them to give their opinion about what they were reading. That is a substantial percentage, even though it was the lowest among the five reasons that online users were asked about. (Number one was getting information on the Web that is not available elsewhere.)[25]

As television edges toward convergence, the Webcast offers a preview of changes in delivering the news. On election night, for example, a station may present its regular programming, with occasional interruptions to update vote totals. On its Web site, it may have anchors and reporters providing political news nonstop. The Webcast anchors, using computers on the news set, may also receive and respond to e-mailed questions and comments from members of the Webcast's audience. All this takes place live—it is real-time news.

Interactivity should not be a gimmick. It should be put to work in ways that enhance responsiveness. If television journalists take seriously the idea of increasing their accountability, the Web will give them a great new opportunity to do something about it. This kind of relationship with the audience may also make good business sense because it can strengthen the ties between news consumers and news providers. Television news organizations have worked hard to maintain "brand loyalty," which has been slipping as more and more news venues become available. Creatively used, Web-based linkages might help tighten these faltering ties.

As video streaming technology improves, news Web sites will regularly carry live coverage of two different kinds of stories: planned events and unplanned breaking news. The former may include meetings of federal, state, and local government bodies (ranging from Congress to school board), trials, and news conferences. Just as news directors decide what stories merit time on a regular newscast, so too will they evaluate events that their Web site might carry. In 1998, for example, the ABC affiliate in Dallas, WFAA, carried a local high-profile murder trial live on its Web site for more than six hours each day for slightly more than two weeks.

From a business standpoint, cross-promotion between Web site and newscast may boost viewership for both. A story on the evening newscast can plug the next day's trial coverage on the Web site, and the Web site can remind its viewers to watch the newscast for a summary of the day's proceedings. This capacity for expanded coverage allows a similarly expanded definition of newsworthiness. By traditional standards, the trial might not deserve such intensive coverage, but with the Web site available and the public interested, offering a gavel-to-gavel Webcast presumably will find viewers. The number of people wanting to watch may not be huge, but news Web sites, as they proliferate, will foster further segmenting of the audience.

Related to this facet of Internet television is another expansion of television news—the development of supplemental cable news channels. On a national level, MSNBC is a good example of this, but most activity in the field is taking place at the local and regional levels. Expanded cable capacity has made more channels available. The news audience is presumed to be large enough to attract advertisers and provide financial sustenance for the news organizations that operate these adjuncts. Part of the theory behind these efforts is the same as the one behind the news Web sites: people want news on demand. Their schedules might not conform to the standard timing of newscasts; work, commuting, responsibilities at home, and other factors create this incompatibility.

In scheduling their newscasts, television news organizations long have implicitly told their audience, "Take it or leave it." CNN was born in part because Ted Turner and his colleagues realized that there were enough people "leaving it" to constitute a sizable audience for an all-news television alternative. Locally, this kind of programming became feasible when Congress gave TV station owners the right to receive payment from cable systems that carried their local broadcasts. As an alternative to direct payment, some cable operators offered television stations extra slots on the cable spectrum, which is where the additional news programming is being placed. Some of the local cable news channels compete directly with broadcast news organizations, and others are purely supplemental, generating their own revenue while promoting the parent's brand identity.[26]

As more of these cable operations are launched, quality will be a concern. Running a twenty-four-hour news operation is expensive, particularly if it includes unique news gathering rather than recycling the parent organization's broadcasts or constantly repeating (with minor updating) the cable organization's own fare. This kind of news programming can be a bare-bones contributor to the bottom line or it can be a substantive contribution to local journalism. Determining which way to go is an important decision for the sponsoring news organization.

In terms of being geared to consumers' varied schedules, all-news television has much in common with Web news sites. As Internet access becomes easier, use of these Web sites will presumably grow substantially. The consumer's ability to check headlines while at work, review a complex story late in the evening, or otherwise get the news when most convenient may dramatically change the relationship between news providers and news consumers.

New chip technology will take this even farther, providing storage capacity for anything coming over air or cable and letting individual consumers retrieve programming when most convenient. The hour-by-hour TV schedule that has dominated life in so many households will become obsolete. News viewers might still watch Peter, Tom, and Dan, but they will do so when they please.

In itself, that does not pose a terrible problem for news organizations. As long as there is an audience and it is receiving commercial messages along with the news content, the timing doesn't matter much. An intrinsic flaw in this is the loss of time-liness. Why should a viewer call up a 6:30 newscast at 10:30 if there is a real-time alternative?

CNN and, more recently, MSNBC were created in anticipation of viewers' evolving expectations of the TV news product. NBC also offers CNBC, which emphasizes business news and presents talk shows featuring Geraldo Rivera, Chris Matthews, and others. CNN proved that it could find a profitable niche in the television news marketplace. CNN chairman Thomas John-son reported that CNN's U.S. channel and its Headline News channel made about $330 million in 1998. That is a far better showing than the "big three" make with their regular newscasts (that is, minus their profitable magazine shows).[27] But CNN's dominance in its field has been eroded by competitors. According to Nielsen Media Research, from October 1994 through September 1995, CNN captured 84 percent of the audience watching cable news. From October 1997 through September 1998, that share shrank to 48 percent, with CNBC and MSNBC together garnering 46 percent and Fox News about 6 percent.[28] That trend has continued.

Television news organizations have been looking over their shoulders at the expanding Internet audience. So far, they have no reason to panic. The December 1998 Pew study found that most Internet users were using the Web "as a mechanism for supplementing, not replacing, their traditional media sources. . . . Three-quarters of heavy online news consumers still get most of their news from traditional print and broadcast news outlets. Almost as many (63 percent) say they use other sources just as much now as they did before getting news online." In addition, "16 percent of heavy online news users use other sources more now than they did before they started getting news online."[29]

There has been some slippage, however, in traditional news consumption. The Pew survey found that "21 percent of Internet users regularly read news stories online instead of reading them in a newspaper or watching them on television." Sixteen percent reported that they were getting more news from online sources than from broadcast and print outlets, and 11 percent said that they were using other sources less than before they had started going online.[30]

Internet news consumers often cite convenience as a major factor in their choice of medium. Interactivity is an important reason for this. The Pew study reported that "substantial numbers of online users turn to the Internet in search of specific information, not just general news. Electronic news organizations have responded to the public's desire for specialized and personalized news by developing mechanisms that allow a small but significant minority to develop their own customized news reports." Eighteen percent of Internet users have news stories e-mailed to them and 17 percent have customized pages for updates about specific news topics.[31]

The television news industry is wisely, if somewhat uncertainly, advancing into new terrain. Cable and the Internet will facilitate a more thorough journalism than television news organizations have offered during the first half century of the profession's existence. More can be better, but only if the increase in quantity is accompanied by a similar commitment to quality.

This commitment must involve more than vague promises to do well. Systemic change will be necessary to ensure that professional responsibility keeps pace with the newest technology.

4

NEWSPAPERS' NEW WORLD

C ompared to the television industry, the newspaper business has responded more quickly and forcefully to the arrival of Internet news vehicles. In part, this is because the traditional paper news industry feels threatened. In 1999 *The
Economist* noted, "Newspapers feel like a natural feature of the
landscape, but they are no more so than canal boats or smoke-
stack factories. Like them, they are the product of a particular
stage of technology." That stage of technology may now be obsolete, and so newspapers, unless they adapt to the new technology, will "vanish, like horse-drawn streetcars, from the scene."[1]
Faced with such dire prospects, the newspapers, presumably,
will feel their survival instincts kick in.

The print media and the Web have something in common:
both rely principally on text, at least until Web technology advances a few notches farther. This means Web sites not only can
deliver a news product that is similar in form to what newspapers offer but also can compete for precious advertising revenues, particularly from classified ads.

The classifieds are perfect for computer sorting and scanning. They constitute one part of the newspaper that is unquestionably more reader-friendly on the computer screen than on
the printed page. But newspapers cannot afford to surrender
this important source of income. For many papers, it constitutes

about 30 percent of revenues, so the papers have no choice but to do battle with the newcomers. Making the struggle more difficult is the array of foes. Classified ads are available as adjuncts to Internet news sites, and some online services exist just to provide classifieds.

The competition for revenue is just one facet of newspapers' expanding online presence. The following is a partial portrait of newspapers online:

- By mid-1999, more than 950 of the roughly 1,600 North American daily newspapers offered online services, including Web sites and partnerships with online companies. That was up from about 750 papers the year before, and 500 papers in 1997.
- Worldwide, more than 2,800 daily, weekly, and other newspapers have online sites.
- The top 100 (by circulation) U.S. newspapers all offer online versions.
- Eighty-two percent of consumers who visit news Web sites also read a newspaper regularly.
- Consumers generally prefer newspapers' Web sites for classified ads, but only 43 percent of respondents to a Newspaper Association of America survey reported that they use newspaper sites as their primary online source of classifieds.
- Visitors to online newspaper sites are considerably more likely than Web users generally to use the Internet for purchases and other financial transactions.[2]

WHAT THE ONLINE NEWSPAPER OFFERS

These figures are evidence of the newspaper industry's commitment to competing for the online audience. Beyond such statistics is the more problematic matter of determining what the online newspaper product should be. Steve Yelvington, editor of the *Minneapolis Star Tribune*'s online version, said, "I have a content prescription that runs around four key points—timeliness, useful, interactive, and entertaining. You'll notice that timeliness is right there at the top."[3]

This emphasis on timeliness underscores the most fundamental change that online capability brings to the newspaper business. Throughout newspaper history, "timely" has been defined in the context of creating a daily product. In exceptional cases, an "extra" edition might be printed for faster reporting of a major, breaking story. But the public came to rely on radio and then especially television for such coverage. Newspapers implicitly accepted this, while emphasizing their own strengths—their breadth and depth of coverage. The culture of the modern news business has been built on this allocation of roles.

With the rise of the Internet and the development of newspapers' online presence, this established order has been pushed aside. Renewed intensity and new rules of the game have come to the competition among news organizations. Public expectations about timeliness have led many newspapers to make parts of their Web sites the equivalent of the Times Square news ticker, where site visitors may glance at the latest bulletins and updates. The Associated Press provides a number of online options to meet this need, just as the AP wire has long supplied more traditional newspaper material. Some print news organizations update their online product every ten minutes throughout the day, assuming that the public is increasingly impatient with anything less than real-time information.

Those who feared the obsolescence of newspapers in a real-time world now have reason to hope that what is obsolete is relying on the printed page as the sole delivery vehicle. The newspaper as journalistic enterprise, rather than as physical product, may have a long life expectancy.

But the newspapers' future will not be easy. Competition with other media will be fierce as the many players define their journalistic roles and restructure their financial foundations. As of early 1999, newspapers had yet to establish themselves as turn-to sources of online information. A survey conducted for Jupiter Communications asked, "Where do you go to access news online?" and elicited the following responses:

Search engines	49 percent
Cable news site	41 percent
Online services	40 percent
Broadcast news site	40 percent
Local newspaper site	30 percent
National newspaper site	24 percent
Other	13 percent
Newsweekly site	12 percent[4]

Newspapers have been trying to define exactly what kinds of local information their readers want online. Movie guides, restaurant listings, school lunch menus, and other such minutiae have had only limited success in attracting an audience. Elon Musk, an executive with software company Zip2, said that newspapers must make their sites sophisticated enough to compete with the major portals. This means, he said, offering free e-mail service, search capabilities, stock quotes, and links to commercial businesses.[5]

Musk's advice makes some sense, but it does not apply in every case. Some newspapers have found that their product itself attracts site visits from far beyond their print readership area. The *San Jose Mercury News*, for instance, reports that 70–80 percent of its Web site audience comes from outside its primary area. Its principal appeal is a substantial amount of business news about the high-tech industry, which it features in its "Good Morning Silicon Valley" feature. Launched in 1996,

GMSV is not only available to those who visit the *Mercury News* site but is also delivered to 38,000 readers via e-mail through Netscape's In-Box Direct service.[6] (This e-mail service is provided by other news organizations as well. It is part of the effort to build "brand loyalty" among readers.)

Online customers like updates, but providing substantive material can be complicated. For a while, GMSV was revised in late afternoon, relying on the paper's print staff to provide copy. Writers, however, resisted taking on this additional task, and the site did not offer enough important breaking news stories to attract a sizable audience. The updating was scrapped after a year.[7]

COMPETITION ONLINE

The experience of the *Mercury News* reflects newspapers' early, careful steps into the world of the Internet. Some of those steps, inevitably, lead in the wrong direction and have to be retraced. But acting in an overly cautious way is ill-advised, since Internet competitors are proliferating and moving aggressively, especially in crucial revenue-producing fields such as advertising. For example, Microsoft's Sidewalk city guides and its Carpoint automobile advertising service compete directly with traditional newspaper offerings. Non-newspaper-based classified services are expected to capture a third of classified ad income within the next few years. If that happens, newspapers will lose more than $6 billion in revenues.[8]

Single newspapers have trouble matching the resources of a powerful company such as Microsoft, so coalitions are forming. Times Mirror, the Tribune Company, and the Washington Post Company created a partnership to offer online classified automobile ads. Classifieds from these three companies' ten large daily papers will greatly outnumber those presented by

Carpoint, and the consortium plans to expand.[9] Similarly, ClassifiedWarehouse.com is a pooled classified venture offering 6 million ads each month, with 400,000 cars and 100,000 jobs advertised on any given day. Classified Ventures is another such operation, pooling ads from 130 newspapers.

One of the most aggressive newspaper players in the online competition is Knight Ridder, America's second largest newspaper publisher. Its thirty-six papers in thirty-four markets reach nearly 10 million readers daily and more than 13 million on Sundays. Online, Knight Ridder's Real Cities is a network of forty Web sites that operates on the following rationale:

> The philosophy of Real Cities is that people on the Internet want quality journalism, a real connection to their community (both geographic and demographic), and information on which they can rely. Many companies and individuals who are attempting to create online communities have primarily a virtual or digital relationship with those communities. Real Cities brings real people and real communities to the Web.[10]

That may sound self-serving, but it underscores an important strength that established news organizations such as Knight Ridder bring into the battle for the Internet audience: a reputation built over the years as a recognized leader in the communities where their papers are published. Will the consumer turn to the hometown newspaper's Web site or rely on Microsoft or some other distant provider? "Distance" may turn out to be meaningless in the era of cybercommunication, but at least at the outset of this era, familiarity may prove to be an asset. Newspapers' principal strength in this respect is their reputation as a source of information that is presented in an orderly way. Columnist Geneva Overholser wrote:

> In any given community, we are the biggest newsgathering operation in town. Nobody can do it the way we do. News-

papers have the editing skills that the new world demands—
the ability to help people make sense out of the exploding
mass of information. And, for all our credibility problems,
we have an imprimatur that people can rely on as they seek
to determine what, out of so much that's available, to believe.[11]

Knight Ridder launched a diverse array of online services,
including city guides; classified ads for homes, cars, and jobs; a
news search engine; online shopping; and other features. Knight
Ridder has more riding on these ventures than many other news
organizations because it is so heavily invested in newspapers.
The corporation sold off its nonprint assets in 1997 and bought
more papers.

The changing economics of the news media confront Knight
Ridder, as a print-oriented business, with a menacing new reality. A third of its $3 billion in revenues comes from classifieds.
Some analysts expect classified advertisers to increase their Web
spending tenfold between 1998 and 2003, a big part of which will
be shifted away from print. Another concern is the hit retail businesses will take from online shopping, which may lead those re-
tailers to reduce their newspaper advertising.[12] A growing share
of retail ads also will move to online locations.

The squeeze comes from many directions. The shift away
from newspapers is already happening. Although newspapers'
ad revenues have been growing, that is a function of the growth
of overall advertising spending. Newspapers' share of the ad
market has actually been shrinking, declining from 24.4 percent
to 21.5 percent between 1993 and 1998, which is a bigger drop
than even network television suffered.[13]

Competition for the online audience is intense as news consumers deal with the vastly expanded information universe the
Internet opens up for them. Readers peruse not only their hometown newspapers—either in traditional or electronic form—but

also papers from throughout the country. Newspapers such as the *New York Times* and *Los Angeles Times* send those who visit their sites e-mail messages about their latest innovations designed to make using their online offerings more enticing.

This diligent courtship of the audience is an essential business strategy. As the novelty of Internet use wears off, surfing is likely to be confined to a much narrower range of sites. Consumers will find their favorite Web destinations and return to them regularly. The sites that survive this shake-out will experience even more intense competition during the next few years.

MAKING MONEY

Another evolving business strategy raises important ethical questions. Advertising on the Internet is becoming a huge and profitable enterprise. At first glance, it appears to be just a variation on the traditional display advertising that is a mainstay of print media. But several new wrinkles have been introduced. First is sponsorship. This has existed for some years; PBS news programs, for example, list their sponsors, and some local television stations sell segments to sponsors. ("Sports is brought to you by . . .") Newspapers, however, have resisted this kind of formalized tie because of wariness about seeming to give an advertiser an ownership stake in editorial content.

That concern is receding, replaced by efforts to bring content and ads closer together. For example, the *Chicago Tribune's* online business section carries a feature about high-tech news called "Silicon Prairie," which has been sponsored by high-tech-related businesses listed as featured advertisers. The news content of the feature is exclusively controlled by the *Tribune*, with no input or review by the advertisers. But when readers see the designation of sponsorship, they might reasonably assume a closeness that could affect what is covered and how it is covered.

Particularly if there is an item about a sponsor's product or service, the objectivity of the reporting might be questioned. Is it a news story or an infomercial? The paper can respond by including in its sponsorship agreement a clause allowing editors to remove the sponsorship identification on days when such stories appear. But over time the association between "Silicon Prairie" and an advertiser will probably (and, from the advertiser's standpoint, desirably) become fixed in readers' minds.[14]

This issue becomes more acute when the online news page includes a link to the sponsor, which usually occurs in feature sections rather than hard news pages. For instance, an online travel section might be sponsored by a travel agency. The reader interested in a particular story can reach the agency through a link on that page. A display ad by the travel agency on the printed page of the newspaper's travel section functions similarly. The advantage for the online sponsor, however, is the prospect of an immediate response from the reader. Given the ease of getting information through the link, that sponsor may well be purchasing a competitive advantage far superior to that which can be acquired by advertising in the traditional print format. That is a fundamental part of the appeal of advertising online.

Complicating the ethics picture is the news organization's stake in this advertising. In 1997, CNN and MSNBC began running ads for Barnes & Noble's online bookselling. The ads offered to sell books related to the news stories that appeared onscreen adjacent to the ads. A story about Russian economic problems, for example, would link to books about post-Soviet Russia. Each book sold through these ads would generate a commission to the site's proprietor.

This relationship between news reporting and product selling is an enticing enough business opportunity to lead to changes in the informal rules governing such ties. CNN even sent Barnes & Noble a daily rundown of top news items to use when choosing what titles it would recommend. Television networks normally do not provide such information to advertisers.[15] Newspapers may offer similar openings to advertisers. The *New York Times* has been criticized for its stake in Barnes & Noble ads with links adjacent to the *Times*'s online book reviews. If a *Times* site visitor bought a book through this link, the *Times* received a commission. This kind of arrangement might create a temptation to review books considered most likely to sell rather than those having literary merit or other noncommercial value.

The larger issue in these matters is far from new: maintaining a wall between editorial and advertising content, separating the journalistic and business sides of the news organization. If the wall is kept in good repair, direct sponsorship of specific news sections might not become common because it would be difficult to create a formula for it that satisfies both editors and advertisers. On the other hand, this wall may be like the Maginot Line: impregnable in theory but inconsequential in practice.

Even before online advertising questions arose, critics detected structural flaws in the wall. Some news organizations, notably the *Los Angeles Times*, opened gateways between news and business managers. The purpose was to focus on improving profits in each section of the paper, counting on ethical self-discipline to prevent conflicts of interest that would infringe on the integrity of the news product. To a certain extent, the instigators of this new relationship are correct in arguing that allowing some news–business contacts will not necessarily cause the entire wall to crumble. But systemic change of this kind introduces structural weakness that makes the long-term existence of the wall problematic.

The nature of the new media necessitates a transition period for many aspects of the relationship between online news provider and advertiser. Setting fees, for example, can be done in several ways. In traditional print advertising, the advertiser pays according to the size of the publication's readership. (This is similar to television ad rates being based on the size and characteristics of viewership as measured by ratings.) The principal basis for online advertising charges is the number of opportunities users have to see the ad, click on it, and visit the advertiser's site. Some variations on this are being tried: actual visits to (rather than opportunities to visit) the advertiser's site and actual transactions, meaning that the advertiser does not pay unless the customer makes a purchase.[16] This variety stems partly from general uncertainty about fee-setting mechanisms and partly from the eagerness of online news providers to procure ads in the early but still highly competitive stages of the online advertising business.

In courting advertisers, some news organizations offer them more than just a place to display their message. For a fee of between $5,000 and $7,500 a year, *Boston Globe* online Help Wanted advertisers would get an "employer profile" page that includes a description of the company, a list of all current job openings, a link to its Web site, and an e-mail link for applicants to submit resumes electronically.[17]

The potential reward for all this effort is huge. Jupiter Communications has predicted that online advertising will total $7.7 billion annually by 2002, a vast increase beyond the revenues generated in the early days of this medium.[18] The Internet Advertising Bureau reported that online advertising revenue reached $1.2 billion in the third quarter of 1999, up from $206.5 million just three years earlier.[19]

The online news industry, like its print, radio, and television siblings, will make most of its money through advertising. But the profits won't come pouring in instantly. Peter Winter, president of Cox Interactive Media, is among those who counsel patience: "Our point of view is that this is long-term brand and franchise building." Citing magazine and television timetables for reaching profitability, he said three to five years would be a reasonable time frame for online news offerings to make money.[20]

For the most part, the industry's early returns have been encouraging. According to a study prepared by the Dataquest research firm in 1999, estimated revenue generated by daily newspapers' Web sites rose from $31.4 million in 1996 to $203.7 million in 1998.[21] However, a 1997 study by NewsLink Associates found as many as 120 papers closing their Web sites, unable to find enough revenue to cover the cost of operating these electronic carriers. At least some of these papers may return in another wave of online ventures when the online financial terrain is smoother.

Even some of the major players who stayed in the game sustained substantial losses. At a December 1998 Paine Webber media conference, the Tribune Company reported losing about $35 million in 1998 on its Web operations, while Knight Ridder lost $23 million. Both these big media companies, like other major players, vowed to continue.[22] The Washington Post Company lost about $63 million on Internet operations in 1999, spending upward of $80 million while generating approximately $17 million in revenue.[23]

The combination of rapidly rising revenues and continued net losses is largely a function of heavy start-up costs. To do online news delivery properly requires a big commitment of personnel and expensive hardware. The companies sustaining early losses can take heart from the experience of a few major news organizations that have already made some money. Among those making a profit in 1999 were Gannett's USAToday.com (the most heavily visited newspaper site) and the Wall Street Journal's wsj.com, which charges a subscription fee.[24]

In pursuit of an online audience, the A. H. Belo Corporation invested in a weather news service. In mid-2000, Belo Interactive, the company's Internet subsidiary (which includes the Web operations of eight daily newspapers, sixteen television stations, and five regional cable news channels) invested in Digital Cyclone. This company's My-Cast personal weather forecasting service provides Web site and e-mail weather information that is updated every three hours about conditions within a three-mile radius. (By comparison, the National Weather Service's forecasts are updated twice a day for a seventeen-mile radius.) Long-range forecasts are also provided, and severe weather alerts are delivered immediately. This will be added to Belo's Web sites and, given the public's intense interest in weather and the appeal of "personalized" forecasts, Belo is likely to see increased traffic on its sites. More traffic means more advertising revenue. This is the kind of specialized, targeted information that news organizations will be adding to distinguish their Web offerings from those of their competitors.

Although advertising remains the preeminent revenue producer, online news products offer unique savings as well. An obvious cost-saving benefit is the nature of the medium itself. Paper is not necessary, an important factor given the cost of newsprint, which reached a high of $658 per metric ton in 1995. Newspapers can also avoid paying carriers and others in their distribution chain, and magazines can save their postage costs.

While the online audience was being cultivated, most newspapers' electronic products were available free. That might not last. Putting online news on a subscription basis is being treated gingerly as the Internet user base grows. Since the level of demand for online news is unknown, news organizations want to set the hook before trying to reel in the customer. Some publications make a sampling of material available to casual site visitors, while reserving the rest for subscribers. Ian Murdock of the *San Antonio Express-News* said of this balancing act, "We need to have enough value for the subscribers, but enough eyeballs for the advertisers."[25]

The *Wall Street Journal* has been among the most assertive in the new field of electronic subscriptions. It raised its annual online subscription rate from $49 to $59 and found few objections. With its print version costing $175 annually, the paper's executives expect some readers to switch from paper to online, but they say they are not worried about excessive changeover within their audience. They can keep raising the online fee to offset revenue losses coming from that shift between versions, and they hope the numbers of online and print subscribers will ultimately be about the same. (The print version had a 1.8 million circulation in early 2000.)[26] By no means is the flow of readers exclusively from print to online. The *New York Times* reports that having a home delivery banner on its Web site has produced an average of 1,400 new subscriptions per month.[27]

Online publications have moved back and forth in how they offer their product. *Slate* magazine, an online venture underwritten by Microsoft, initially was available free, then began charging $19.95 for a year's subscription, while still offering teaser pages free. After attracting 25,000 subscribers at this rate, all of *Slate* again became free. The reason: for each subscriber, ten to fifteen people were visiting the free pages. Editor Michael Kinsley said this helped push ad revenues to the point at which the magazine could again be offered at no charge.[28]

In exchange for not charging an access fee, the site may ask visitors to register by providing zip code, gender, income, and other information of interest to advertisers. The *New York Times* gathers this kind of information but promises privacy, reporting the data to advertisers in aggregate and not individually. But other site owners might sell personalized information, and advertisers could then direct personalized e-mail and other solicitations to the registrants.

People are becoming accustomed to getting news free on the Internet. In 2000, Princeton Research Associates conducted a survey for Web content provider screamingmedia.com, which found that 89 percent of the respondents had never paid for news or other information on the Web, and 83 percent were not willing to pay. The respondents cited frequent updates and news that is not available elsewhere as principal attractions of the Internet.[29]

Yet another source of revenue is a publication's archives. Serious researchers can subscribe on a monthly or yearly basis, but people looking for a single story can search the online archive, almost always for free, paying only if they find a story they want to read (and perhaps print). Most papers offering this service charge several dollars per story. It may never be a huge money-maker, but once the newspaper has its back issues accessible on the Web, it has a source of extra income. The newspaper must deal with billing (usually done by credit card) or may use an agent to manage its archive operation.

These are the large and small pieces of a new industry within an industry. Determining which to keep and refine and which to discard will take some time. But clearly, even in the earliest stages of newspapers' online experience, money can be made from this part of the news business.

RUNNING THE ONLINE NEWSPAPER

The place of online news within the larger news organization has yet to be fully defined. Is the online product merely an add-on, like a new section of the paper, or is it truly a separate entity? If the latter, what level of operational autonomy should it be granted? More specifically, issues of staffing, editorial supervision, production schedules, and other mundane but essential matters demand thoughtful decisions. Those who run news organizations must determine the best ways to take advantage of the unique characteristics of their online product in order to enhance its journalistic and profit-making potential.

At one end of the spectrum the paper product is eliminated and replaced with a Web-only newspaper. Utah's *Orem Daily*

Journal did just that. The paper's reporters keep doing their jobs much as they did in the past, and online ads generate revenue. This is not necessarily a path other papers will follow. The Orem paper is a special case: it was created in 1998 with a plan to make it an exclusively online product as soon as a subscriber base was established by a print version.[30] But the *Daily Journal's* evolution certainly will provoke some thinking.

Most newspapers are organizing dual operations. For them, a starting point may be deciding where to put the online operation. Some news organizations have made their online staff part of the newsroom mainstream, while others have placed it elsewhere, sometimes not even in the same building. Such segregation is usually attributed to logistics. Anyone who has spent time in newsrooms knows that space is always at a premium and that protests are loud whenever new equipment or people are squeezed in. Asking someone to give up or share a desk is the equivalent of declaring war. The path of least resistance may be to set up the online shop in its own quarters.

That approach might appear to be the most convenient, but it carries a price. The news consumer should be able to assume that the online product's offerings draw from the entirety of the news organization's news-gathering process. But keeping online staff members in their own high-tech bastion may work against that. Being part of the newsroom lets the online journalist benefit from colleagues' input. Doing good journalism requires understanding the nuances of a story—background, relative credibility of sources, what was included and excluded and why, and so forth. Give-and-take among journalists is part of that process. Without this kind of grounding, the online staff operates at a disadvantage and the electronic product is likely to be a copy of the print story or even an inferior version of it.

If the online newspaper is to possess its own vitality and attract its own following, it must do better than that. Stressing the importance of the quality of the online product, David Blackwell, deputy managing editor of the Fort Lauderdale *Sun-Sentinel*, said, "The bottom line is that our site needs to reflect the offerings of a 370-person editorial staff and not just the work of a dozen producers and online editors."[31]

Particularly when breaking news is being reported, full integration of print and online journalists is a good idea. The flow of news onto the Web should be as smooth and as fast as possible, and should not have to pass from the main newsroom to a separate online newsroom before being made available to the Internet audience. That kind of routing defeats one of the main purposes of having a news Web site. As online competition intensifies, being quickest will be increasingly prized.

Apart from breaking news, coverage that can be scheduled will benefit from smooth collaboration between print and online staffs. Writers preparing stock market reports for a morning paper may have a deadline of about 8:00 P.M. With an online edition, they might have an additional late afternoon deadline for the Web version's readers. As newsrooms adjust their schedules to incorporate the needs of an online news product, there certainly will be objections from reporters, who generally are quick to feel oppressed. On closer examination, however, they probably are not being asked to do much extra work but just to change the form of their work product. It will take some time before the newsroom culture adapts to the demands of the electronic news schedule, but this task is far from insurmountable.

At 1:00 P.M. each day, washingtonpost.com publishes its "PM Extra" that updates stories from the morning edition (which has already been updated as events warrant) and presents five to ten stories from the *Post*'s newsroom. Mark Stencel, politics editor of washingtonpost.com, said:

> We're effectively putting out another edition of the newspaper on the Web. That has also led to additional filings from the newsroom throughout the afternoon and even after

deadline. . . . These are news reports about stories that happen too late to get into the print edition of the newspaper,
and sometimes they may be of interest, but not enough interest to carry them into the following day's newspaper.[32]

During the 2000 presidential campaign, the online *Post* featured
"E-mail from the Trail"—fresh reports from correspondents
traveling with the candidates.

The flexibility that comes with newness pervades virtually
every part of the online news operation, including the definition
of "online journalist." When a newspaper advertises for an online staff member, the qualifications listed may differ from those
of a traditional journalist. Instead of emphasizing just a talent
for news gathering and writing, the online job description may
require experience with Adobe's Illustrator and Photoshop,
Macromedia Flash, audio and video editing, scripting processes,
and other such skills that many old-line journalists have probably never even heard of. The person holding this kind of job is
often referred to as a "producer," which has been a position in
television and radio, not print. Thus the online news business
has created a new occupational genre that involves both gathering the news, usually not firsthand, and presenting it on the Web
site.

How much traditional journalism experience this requires
is being debated, particularly in terms of who makes journalistic
decisions. Technical skills are important in the online news operation, but it is important to remember that much of journalism
is a function of judgment: what is important, what is accurate,
how much corroboration and background are needed. "Tech-
ies," no matter how bright, might not have the training and experience to make those calls.

That is why skills-based segregation in the online newsroom is risky. Ideally, the traditional reporter and the new-
generation producer will soon work closely together. Rich Meis-

lin, editor of the *New York Times on the Web*, has noted that so far there has not been much movement from the print version to the online product: "The people who are reporters at the newspaper probably wouldn't find the producer-level jobs interesting because there's not a lot of reporting to them."[33] Offsetting that, however, are the higher salaries from some Web properties and the allure of participating in a revolution.

That will change as online news operations do more original reporting. A survey conducted by public relations and marketing firm Middleberg and Associates that was released in mid-1999 found that newspaper Web sites offering less than 5 percent original content had declined from 39 percent in 1997 to 27 percent in 1998. Don Middleberg, the firm's chairman, said, "News organizations have clearly broken away from the trend to use Web sites solely as a delivery tool. They've begun treating them as a new medium." As evidence of this, Middleberg cited the survey finding that nearly a third of the respondents integrate multimedia components—mainly audio and video recordings—into their Web articles.[34]

Another major change for newspapers is taking advantage of interactivity. This too is something of a cultural shift for an institution that has traditionally dictated its own terms for its contacts with the public. But aloofness will not sit well with a cyberaudience that expects to use the Internet for true back-and-forth communication, not merely one-way transmitting or receiving.

Although print news media have done far better than television and radio in correcting errors and publishing letters to the editor, additional accountability is always possible. Some newspapers have begun printing reporters' e-mail addresses (and sometimes phone numbers) at the end of stories in their online and print editions. One of the papers doing this is the Raleigh, North Carolina, *News & Observer*, whose online managing editor, Norman Cloutier, said: "I think one of the best things about the policy is what it does for the paper's credibility. Simply seeing a name and phone number or e-mail at the end of every story makes the newspaper seem much more accountable. Even if you never call or write, I think it has an impact."[35] Those journalists who do not yet provide e-mail addresses may soon find themselves compelled to do so by their audience's changing expectations. Once news consumers get a taste of improved access, they will likely want more.

The evidence so far is mostly anecdotal, but early indications are that readers are taking advantage of electronic access. Perhaps the ease of sending e-mail (no envelope, no stamp, no trip to the mailbox) is part of the appeal. Whatever the reason, journalists are finding the flow of communication from readers increasing. There is some griping and sniping, but many of the e-mail messages contain thoughtful comments and questions and offer useful tips for further stories.

Sometimes these e-mail messages from readers point out errors. Making corrections online is still a work in progress. A survey conducted in 1998 by Jackie Chamberlain of the *Riverside Press-Enterprise* found that "there are no standards for identifying, correcting, and editing the errors in newspaper Web editions."[36] Chicago journalist Frank Sennett started Slipup.com to draw attention to online publications' corrections policies (or lack of policies). Sennett said that

> every news site should provide readers with a prominent link to its corrections page. That link might be a standing one—always present in the same spot on the homepage or in the table of contents—making the corrections section easier for readers to find. . . . To work effectively, the correction process must be a two-step one in which news sites prominently acknowledge mistakes when they are discovered, and then append the original story file with a note updating the material. This is a better approach than simply erasing errors from a story file, which smacks of a mistake-hiding rewrite of history.[37]

Online stories, like any published material, can take on a life of their own, especially when they are electronically clipped and pasted and sent flying through cyberspace to new recipients, who may save it in their files or paste it into their own publications. As with other media, corrections should be made as swiftly as possible and should be designed to undo any damage that might have been done by the error. Even good-faith efforts cannot rectify every mistake's aftereffects, but at least some of the news audience may take note when the attempt is made.

Another facet of the electronic news product is the ability to measure with considerable precision what the audience is most interested in. When the reader selects a page from the on-screen index or menu, the cyberturnstile clicks. For television sites, this is a more sophisticated version of the ratings that have been so important to the TV news business almost since its inception. For newspapers, however, this is something new. Print news organizations' audience research has been conducted mostly through surveys and focus groups. Now the number of readers turning to each story can be counted.

There is a potential downside to this. A convenient quantitative measure of relative popularity of the site's offerings could tempt news managers to eliminate or reduce coverage of topics attracting the fewest visits. Why pay to have your own reporters or even wire services produce stories few people care about? Doing away with "unpopular" stories may be good business, but it may well be bad journalism because it probably would mean a narrowing of the scope of coverage. Much foreign news, for example, may attract a readership that looks puny compared to the numbers who flock to crime stories or to weather and sports reports. But to significantly reduce or even discontinue that coverage would be a great disservice to those readers who count on the news organization to open at least a small window on the rest of the world. Resisting the temptation to make that kind of alteration in the scope of coverage will be one of the new responsibilities for news organizations that join the ranks of on-line providers.

A larger systemic issue facing all online news organizations is devising a news delivery schedule. How often and how thoroughly will news be updated? Answers will depend on various factors, including cost and audience expectations, for example, during the sick-out (a de facto strike) by many American Airlines pilots in February 1999. Particularly in cities where American is a principal provider of air service, a sizable number of people wanted to know which flights were cancelled, how long the work stoppage was likely to last, and other such matters. The airline's own Web site provided a list of cancelled flights, updated hourly, but nothing about progress or lack of progress in ending the disruption. In pre-Internet days, the public would have to wait for regularly scheduled television and radio newscasts to learn the latest information, but the advent of news Web sites meant (or was expected by news consumers to mean) that information would be available on demand.

That was not, however, always the case. The emerging online news business had not yet devised a smooth, consistent mechanism for making available this kind of information. Some newspaper sites had just that day's stories from the paper on the site, with an update available only by clicking on a wire service link. Some other sites did better, periodically remaking their online "front page" to detail the latest cancellations and other new items about the story, such as progress in getting the pilots back to work.

Providing that kind of information is not intrinsically difficult, but it does require a news manager's decision to do it and a commitment of personnel to provide the updates at regular intervals. Ideally, from the news consumer's standpoint, the ongoing coverage would feature reports at least every few hours and would include a prominent notice about when the next update would appear on the site. That could disrupt the flow of news preparation for the regular print or electronic product unless extra staff members are assigned to the updating. Designing this process requires some thought.

Washingtonpost.com offered a good example of intensive real-time coverage in April 2000 during protests in Washington, D.C., against the World Bank and International Monetary Fund. In addition to the main story, which was updated minute by minute when events dictated, the site offered audio dispatches from reporters; video; and a gallery of still photos, maps, and lists of street and business closings; background material about the protests; a live online discussion with an economist; message boards for readers to offer their opinions about the disruption and police response; and more. For the *Post*, this was a local as well as a national and international news story. With twenty reporters covering the protests throughout the city, the paper and particularly its online version proved how the Web lets a newspaper challenge radio and television in covering a breaking story.

Perhaps not many stories will merit such intensive treatment, but news organizations should recognize that their audience's expectations will rise as the Internet becomes more widely used as a source for news. The adjustment to this might be especially difficult for newspapers that have become accustomed to life without much direct competition. Most American cities now have only one major daily paper. Although these papers compete with television and radio news organizations, their medium has its own comfortable, competition-free niche.

Among news Web offerings, however, the audience is likely to ignore such distinctions and patronize the news sites that give them what they want when they want it. Television news organizations may be better equipped to deal with this because they are used to the intense head-to-head competition between stations and networks that most newspapers have not faced for years. The stakes in this are enormous, since news consumers almost certainly will settle into patterns of Web site visiting, just as they have developed patterns of reading certain newspapers and magazines and watching certain television channels. A site deemed by the audience to fall short might never recapture a lost audience.

Journalistic creativity can flourish on the Web. A report about a president's speech can offer video of all or parts of the speech. A story about competing candidates can offer their detailed voting records or responses to an issues questionnaire. Coverage of a fire can be supplemented with a map of the area and a link to any record of previous fire safety violations.

Deciding what supplemental material to provide is only part of the Web journalist's task. How to present it—usually in a nontraditional, nonlinear way—also requires imagination. In its coverage of the 1996 presidential debates, washingtonpost.com carried the full transcript of the debates with a cartoon referee throwing a penalty flag at certain points. Readers who clicked on the referee could read the *Post*'s truth-testing analysis of what may have been an error in the candidate's statement.[38]

This kind of attention-getting device could be supplemented by audio or video clips of the questioned passage, a link to a chat room in which reporters discussed the debate, and links to outside information sources (partisan and nonpartisan). This may be more than most news consumers want, but providing lots of information is a key part of news Web sites' appeal.

Timeliness is another Web asset that newspaper sites should take full advantage of. An audience conditioned by years of television and radio news will not be satisfied with online sites that feature new technology but the old news cycle schedule. If a big story breaks in the morning, the newspaper site simply must deliver current reporting. Covering breaking news has not been part of the newspaper's traditional role, but the Web has changed that role.

Besides speed, a news Web site can offer personalized information. At some news sites, visitors can enter their zip codes and get information about their elected officials, local schools, entertainment listings, and other such information. That precision may be the key to the Internet's ultimate triumph as news provider. People will want it, and only the Web will provide it.

Newspapers and their Web sites will face challenges to their journalistic skill and their imagination during their shakedown voyage on the Internet. The difficulties are not insurmountable, but they will not simply resolve themselves. They are largely problems of process, and their solution will require a mix of good management and good journalism.

5

ADVENTURES IN CONVERGENCE

As print and electronic news organizations have developed their presence on the World Wide Web, they have, for the most part, retained primary identities that are based in their respective media. Washingtonpost.com, for example, is clearly a journalistic subsidiary of the *Washington Post* newspaper. Sometimes there is blurring of primacy, as with MSNBC on the air and MSNBC online, but so far this is the exception, not the rule.

So far. Separation among the three principal news media—print, television/radio, and Internet—might not prove sensible or even feasible in the long run. Some new amalgam of the three may evolve as their technologies of news delivery come together. This will be the future: convergence.

USER-FRIENDLY TECHNOLOGY

As an exercise in word association, saying "Internet" leads to "computer." Saying "computer" produces an image of the desktop machine, drab or stylish, that is now a part of so many offices and homes. That word-and-image linkage is nicely simple, but it is rapidly becoming outdated.

Some of the functions of the computer—particularly the home computer—are being replaced by "information appliances." These include cell phones that offer touch-screen Web access and a combination nine-inch television, CD player, and Web browser that can be attached to the bottom of a kitchen cabinet (and will be distributed by a kitchen appliance company). The handheld computer is evolving rapidly, making the early versions of the popular Palm obsolete. The personal computer is moving from desk to pocket.

The union of cell phones and the Internet promises to be a lasting one, although evidence of this is not yet as common in the United States as it is elsewhere. The U.S. wireless phone industry has lagged behind the European one and even farther behind the one in Japan. In early 2000, DoCoMo, Japan's leading cell phone company, was gaining new customers at the rate of 25,000 a day largely because of the appeal of its "I-mode" service. I-mode phones have full-color display screens, recognize voice commands, and have plug-in keyboards for users who want to write long e-mail messages. Coming soon will be high-quality streaming audio and video. While the American and European Wireless Application Protocol uses text services bundled together by the cell phone companies, the DoCoMo service provides full access to the Web.[1]

The key for all these devices, and for the future of Internet use, is "transparency"—use of the Web as an integral part of daily life. As technology improves and Internet access and use become faster and easier, people will go online as part of their everyday routine, not even thinking about it—much like making telephone calls or switching on the television. When this comes about, the Web will be used increasingly for mundane tasks such as getting weather forecasts, checking movie theater schedules, getting traffic reports, and anything else that people want with the least amount of trouble. International Data Corporation has estimated that by 2001, sales of information appliances will outnumber those of home PCs, with the gap between the two growing as ease of use increases and prices decline.[2] These new devices will be particularly popular once Internet access is easier. Fiber-optic cable will allow a telephone line to serve dual purposes: standard voice communication and "always-on" connection to the Internet. No more of the dial-up pinging and busy signals that can discourage Web use. Communication companies are rushing to make this the new standard.

Presumably, this easier access to the Internet will affect news consumption. In addition to quick hits for nuggets of information, checking the news might become more of a habit. For many people, this will not be a substantial commitment to get detailed background material but just a check to make sure the local community and the world are still in one piece. News organizations must make such news presentation accessible and interesting. Ideally, it will entice the consumer to dip deeper into the reservoir of information, either at first visit or later. The easier the access and the more user-friendly the news site, the more likely it becomes that the rate of online news consumption will increase.

Jupiter Communications, which monitors computer use, predicts that 56 percent of American homes will be connected to the Internet by 2002, up from 32 percent in early 1999 (with even higher percentages for offices). Internet service provider Earth-Link Network, Inc., reports that although today's Internet users may spend forty hours a month online, that figure could rise to 200 hours per month once Web use becomes more transparent.[3] Given the explosive growth of Internet use, these estimates may be conservative. On the business side, advertisers will be taking note of such changes, and ad revenues will fuel expanded offerings on the Web.

Internet use is being transformed from a high-tech exercise that many find daunting to just another convenience—a tremendous breakthrough. As this proceeds, the first decade of the new millennium may prove to be as important to the rise of the Internet as the 1950s were to the acceptance of television as an integral part of American life.

Part of this evolution will be a function of a convergence of hardware. The conventional wisdom to date has decreed that no one wants to "watch" a PC like a television. With its extra pieces (keyboard, monitor, and speakers), the personal computer is a useful but clunky device, and the logistics of its use generally run counter to the transparency that makers of information appliances hope to foster.

That problem is waning as computer equipment becomes less cumbersome (e.g., thinner monitors) and as Internet connections become smoother. These two factors are crucial in the convergence of television and the Internet because they enhance "streaming"—transferring data, including video and audio, in a continuous stream, rather than in a file that must be downloaded. This is the process by which live news coverage is delivered on the Web. It also will be used by corporations to carry speeches, seminars, and other content on what can be the equivalent of an in-house television/Web network. These businesses can also reach their customers this way. Some brokerages offer online "newscasts," with their own analysts reporting about the markets and touting their services. With streaming, anyone with an adequate computer or other "information appliance" will be able to watch a newscast—whatever the species—live. The traditional television set will not be necessary.

Among its other attributes, this technology allows remote access to local television. Travelers, for example, wherever they may be, can watch streamed newscasts from their hometowns if they want to do so. All they need is Internet access. In its early stages, this kind of video has been flawed by its choppy flow and occasional interruptions. These are transient problems that will be erased by new generations of modems and improved Internet connections.

Radio is another growing presence on the Internet, also

through streaming. The Web's appeal to radio stations and Net-only audio suppliers is largely economic; much of the expensive technology of a broadcast station is unnecessary for the delivery of audio on the Net. This works to the benefit of listeners, since fewer costs mean fewer ads. Also, Web radio is interactive, allowing listeners to chat electronically while listening, read information about the music being played, or order a recording of what they are hearing.

Radio news on the Web possesses much of the same appeal as television carried on the Internet. It can be accessed through a computer when no radio is available, and local radio stations can be listened to from remote places. For the American traveling in Europe who wants to listen to his or her hometown baseball team's game, streaming audio on the Web is a simple way to do so.

As with video, streaming audio still has problems of sound quality and sometimes stalled flow, but many stations are nevertheless streaming their audio to build an audience as technical shortcomings are worked out. Worldwide, thousands of radio stations have begun doing this. Aficionados of foreign news and foreign music can spend countless hours electronically traveling the globe.

The next step for radio is the Internet-only station. An early example is WTOP2.com, a twenty-four-hour all-news station created by WTOP AM/FM in Washington, D.C., and the Associated Press. With its own news director and technical staff, WTOP2 initially used WTOP and AP material, later expanding to provide some unique coverage.[4]

Web radio will certainly have its users, but more intriguing are the prospects for Web television. Computer technology companies are producing the hardware that allows the television viewer to put on his or her screen an array of images simultaneously—fare from regular TV channels, Web sites, videocassettes, digital video discs (DVD), and anything else that is suited for a television or computer screen. Living room electronics will steadily grow smarter.

During news coverage, viewers can create their own visual context for stories as they are aired, mixing video, still photos, and text. The convergence here will be found in the format similarities of news organization sites, regardless of the original media of those organizations. In terms of ability to provide mixed media news coverage, what providers such as ABC News and the *New York Times* offer separately will be little different in format, and their initial joint efforts may well expand into a more complete partnership. But then, as now, it will be up to each news organization to make editorial judgments about what it will deliver to online consumers. Those judgments will be more complex than they are today. On any given day, ABC may want to offer supporting text to back up video from a story; the *Times* may decide to use video as part of some of its stories.

Technological convergence will not, in itself, impose bland similarity on the products news organizations offer. Other than the expanded range of format options, how news decisions are made—the journalistic criteria used to determine what gets covered and how—will not differ much from today's editorial process. The quality of journalism will still be important and will distinguish any one news site from its competitors.

MAKING CONVERGENCE WORK

Journalists who deliver the news online work in several ways. Some redo material that has been published in another venue, such as a newspaper or a television newscast. Others are devoted to creating the online news product. Virtually all of these people, who are doing serious journalism, consider themselves members of the same profession. There are, however, some differences in the way they do their jobs.

How their audiences get the news is a factor in these differences. A significant number of online news consumers go online at the workplace. That environment affects expectations about the news product. Time pressures may force Web readers to check only the top of a story, maybe coming back to the rest later. The teasing leads that are much in vogue in newspaper writing today may elicit impatience from the workplace news consumer.

For audience members who have the time and inclination to use online news for in-depth journalism, a nonlinear approach might work best. Readers will survey the array of relatively short blocks of text and then choose those that most interest them. From these blocks, they can proceed to links—electronic digressions that amplify the elements of the basic story. The task for the online journalist is to provide enough solid information (meaning that it has been verified and merits the imprimatur of the news organization) and then offer the news consumer access to additional material through internal and external links. The former might include a connection to the news organization's own archives, and the latter might offer an array of primary and secondary sources that were used in the writing of the original story.

Online journalistic style will develop swiftly, shaped by the demands of the market and the evolution of the newsroom. Meanwhile, a significant impact of the Internet on journalism across the board will be found in its use as a research tool. Particularly for smaller news organizations that don't have their own extensive research libraries, Web sites and e-mail provide almost unlimited avenues to background research and sources. This research capability is spawning its own quasi-journalistic industry among the access providers that try to bring some order out of the vast and in some respects chaotic universe of Web offerings. A tool such as thebighub.com provides access to thousands of searchable online databases. A reporter merely types in a topic and the search mechanism provides a list of relevant sites.

Another factor for all journalists to consider is the speed of reaction—individual and collective—fostered by the Internet. As a major story unfolds, Web chat rooms are likely to be crowded with attendees ready to expound on the events at hand. As Lisa Napoli observed in the *New York Times*, these cyber gathering places for expressing opinions make the Net "the soapbox—and barroom—of our times."[5] These forums do not affect how basic reporting is done, but for journalists they open a window on public sentiment.

Chat rooms can be useful to journalists in fashioning further coverage, but only in a decidedly unscientific way. Ease of access to chat room discourse is alluring, but sampling chat room sentiment should not be considered a legitimate replacement for properly done opinion polling. Chat rooms may attract people who are simply interested in the news or those with a common interest or ideology. Unlike the letters to the editor section of a newspaper, some chat rooms permit anonymity.

Particularly until Internet use becomes much more widespread, journalists should keep in mind that the online constituency differs significantly from the overall population. A Pew Research Center study of online polling (conducted in October 1998) found "significant attitudinal differences between the general public and those who participate in online polls." Although the Internet user base is steadily expanding, this group (especially the true devotees) is still younger, better educated, and more affluent than the overall American population.[6] Similarly, e-mail discussion lists can provide useful insight into opinions and agendas but, again, these lists by definition encompass relatively narrow constituencies. Journalists who are intrigued by the Internet as a wellspring of information need to bear in mind that, although the Internet's value in this regard is indisputable, like any source, it is far from flawless.

Those who are doing new media journalism are likely to develop an affinity for their medium, and this might influence the selection of story topics and the intensity of coverage. In 1999, when the Justice Department brought an antitrust suit against the Microsoft Corporation, online news coverage was more extensive and more regularly updated than that provided by traditional media news organizations. The reporting was also more creative, using the Net's capabilities to good advantage. The online version of the *San Jose Mercury News* offered a "virtual courtroom" that allowed readers to click for information about witnesses, evidence, and other material relating to the trial. ZDNet News updated its coverage as often as four times a day. Nonjournalistic sources also used the Web. Both Microsoft and the Department of Justice had Web sites providing information about the trial from their respective perspectives.[7]

News consumers interested in this trial could thus pick and choose from among objective and not-so-objective sources of information. In addition, they had to decide which of these sources deserved trust, distrust, or something in between. Given the vast volume of material available on the Internet, determining the trustworthiness of online information is a daunting challenge, but the medium's fundamental characteristics may foster self-policing. Interactivity expert Edwin Schlossberg wrote:

> The astonishing speed and connectivity of the Internet provides the opportunity for the online community to become more adept at evaluating the truth of what they are told, the meaning of what they see, and the conclusions that can be drawn from the material. If a scientist fakes an experiment and posts the results on the Internet, many other scientists will test it and will immediately post their own results. That's the way it should work with all ideas. This kind of collective response expands all our knowledge simultaneously.[8]

Although its newness dazzles, the Web really is little different from other media in terms of its potential to abuse and be abused and its capability for self-governance. If its quality and standards are taken for granted, a journalistic and ethical mess will certainly be the result. If, on the other hand, the medium receives the thoughtful attention that its potential merits, many problems can be resolved. In late 1998, the Online News Association was formed to evaluate the unique and shared responsibilities of this form of journalism. The group's members, many of whom are veterans of other media, plan to address topics such as ethics and journalism education.

INTERACTIVITY—NEXT STEPS

Traditional delivery of news is a one-way process. The news organization sends—on paper or electronically—and the public receives. Aside from a few avenues such as letters to the editor, no communication flows the other way.

Online media can change that. Instead of just publishing, news organizations will be able to *converse* with their audience. If they fail to do so, if they fail to make the new media more responsive than the old, they will be making a serious mistake. As the Internet becomes more widely used in other, non-news-related ways, the public will better understand interactivity and will come to expect it. Online sites that do not take full advantage of it will almost certainly be relegated to second-tier status in terms of use and trust.

For news organizations, interactivity can and should be much more than a public relations gimmick. Already, there is a tilt toward flash over substance on some news Web sites. Many of these sites offer visitors a chance to participate in a "poll." The visitor answers the question of the day ("Should the President be impeached?" or "Which movie will win the Best Picture Oscar?"), the visitor votes with a click, and in a few seconds receives the up-to-the-minute tabulation of answers. With no control over the sample, this is a poll only in a loose, unscientific sense.

Also in the self-promotion category, the stars of some news organizations have their own Web sites, offering biographies and favorite recipes, as well as personal e-mailboxes. If the journalists take the trouble to engage in real give-and-take, responding thoughtfully to queries, the e-mail can be helpful. But if only canned responses and thinly disguised advertising are sent back to the audience, this exchange is worth little.

One interactive venue certain to become more widely used is the chat room. This allows collective, rather than just one-to-one, contact between journalists and public. Reporters can discuss the content of stories and the news-gathering techniques they used. Editors can electronically chat about newsroom policies and decision making. This might win some new friends for the news media, and at the very least could help dispel some of the suspicions many people have about the press. If journalists see their role as shining a searchlight on institutions of power in society, it follows that they should be willing to illuminate their own practices. Chat rooms and other interactive Web capabilities provide excellent opportunities for doing this. At the very least, every substantive news story and opinion column should include the writer's e-mail address.

Even as daily news providers are expanding their offerings, magazines are also embracing the Web in order to keep pace with real-time news providers. *Money* magazine, which publishes on paper monthly, offers a full calendar of daily updated material—financial news, columns, research, and more. Some of the magazine's journalists respond to e-mailed questions every day. *Money* also provides online services to help site visitors evaluate stocks, check interest rates, buy a car, and so on. The market is driving this; just appearing monthly is no longer competitive.

In every aspect of the news organization's online product,

the primary commitment should be to news content. This is not just a call for journalistic responsibility as an esoteric matter of principle. The arrival of the new media brings with it the need to reassert some old journalistic functions. First among these is the exercise of editorial discretion. With an almost infinite supply of information flowing through the Internet, the public may have greater need for the filter of journalistic judgment and standards to help sift through the mass and separate news from propaganda and falsehood. Intellectual anarchy can thrive in cyberspace. The Web has already provided fertile ground for rumor.

Easy to use and pervasive in its reach, the Internet amplifies speech. That is a wonderful thing when it means bringing truth to people who have been deprived of it. But it is far less wonderful when the Web's messages are false or filled with hate. One of the news media's traditional roles has been arbitrating public discourse. That task is even more important in the cyberage.

There will be much debate about policing the Web. Pornography and protection for children have been the biggest initial concerns, and legal measures are being designed to address them. But what should be done about a neo-Nazi Web site that provides bomb-making instructions? Should a news organization that does a story about this group and its Web site provide a link to it? Would this be an appropriate adjunct to the news story, to let the public see for itself what the issue is, or would the link only amplify hatred?

As convergence takes place, all news organizations, regardless of their original venue, will have to redefine their ethical duties in accordance with the demands of evolving news technology. Stepping into cyberspace means taking on responsibilities that may have received little notice previously. Television stations, for example, might provide a forum for their audience by formalizing their letters to the executive producer policy and allotting space for it on their Web site. Newspapers will need to address issues related to video content (such as graphic violence) when they offer it on their sites.

Convergence will be accompanied by a collapse of the walls separating the various news media in terms of their distinct professional ethics. It also will change the public's expectations about how much news will be available. Television has long excused the lack of depth in most of its news offerings by pleading format limitations. In the Internet era, that excuse will no longer be credible.

The material on a Web site does not materialize by itself. News organizations will have to make important decisions about the level of resources they are willing to put into expanding their news product. This issue encompasses everything from hiring foreign correspondents to increasing the number of subscriptions to wire services and syndicated sources. For local news organizations, it involves reaching more constituencies within the local community.

Targeted news may become much more common. Residents of individual neighborhoods will be able to get information about the people and events in which they are most interested. From hard news to community bulletin boards, news organizations will easily be able to offer precisely localized material. This might include crime reports, stories about neighborhood schools and community groups, event calendars, and other such information that is on the mundane side of the news spectrum. Newspapers don't have the space and television and radio don't have the time to publish this material, but those constraints vanish on the Web. Gathering this information will require some effort (more clerical than journalistic), but posting it on the Web site may increase the overall number of visits. This is the stuff of daily life. Most people are more interested in a neighborhood crime report than in the latest speculation about the future of the Middle East. But pull the audience into the tent with the former, and they might stay for the latter. And once in the tent, they will also be seeing ads.

Targeting can be even more precise, with an online news product specially designed for each member of the audience who wants one. Pointcast.com, for example, invites its users to design their own news pages featuring coverage from various news organizations that is automatically updated. CNN similarly offers its users a checklist of general news topics, such as stories about specific countries and sports reports about specific teams. CNN then presents a daily personalized news digest based on those selections.

This precise targeting might prove effective in attracting people who complain that the news media tell them too much about topics in which they have no interest. This disaffected audience, which frightens news executives with its large and growing ranks, might be recaptured with a product that is carefully tailored to meet their individual interests. An expanded, individually categorized audience will also be attractive to advertisers and thus may boost the news organization's revenues.

On the other end of the spectrum of audience involvement with the news, the Internet may turn news consumers into news reporters. This is not a new idea. Ever since home film and video cameras arrived on the scene, television stations have used amateur footage of events they have not been able to cover themselves, for example, the home video of a tornado bearing down on a community. Another version of this is the "MTV News Unfiltered" feature, which encouraged viewers to submit story ideas and provided a selected few with camcorders to produce their own news spots for airing on the network's show. It is even easier for a news organization to add such contributions to their online offerings, particularly as digital cameras and other consumer-friendly hardware make electronic transmission of material more feasible. At the very least, news organizations can make Web site space available for audience members to submit their own reviews of movies, restaurants, books, and anything else they want to comment on. This enormously expands the letters to the editor column concept. With that participation may come new interest in the overall news product.

In addition to submitting material to established news organizations, some people may want to become self-made journalism entrepreneurs. They can set up their own Web sites featuring their own version of the news, complete with their own audio and video. Finding a sizable audience is another matter, but perhaps the whole news process will seem less forbidding and less distant if doing journalism becomes a more commonplace enterprise.

The extent of interactivity is limited only by the extent of imagination. As traditional news media converge on the common ground of the Internet, their futures will be determined partly by how efficiently they remove the long-standing barriers between themselves and their audience. The Web will not be the property of journalists or any media organizations; it will belong to everyone. The sense of autonomy arising from that is the essence of an interactive medium.

CONVERGING PROFITS

Almost all of the online news business is being built in unknown territory. How big the audience will be, what intermedia competition will be like, where revenues will come from—these and other issues make developing the new media a high-stakes gamble, even for the most venerable news corporations.

So far the trend has been for most news organizations, regardless of their principal medium, to launch online ventures. In many large cities, the newspaper(s) and local television stations have Web sites that compete with one another in traditional ways. Even their audiences are derived from the parent organizations. All of them charge ahead, trying to keep pace with technology advances and audience expectations.

The field is likely to narrow simply because no market—national or local—can sustain so many news Web sites, at least not until the science of Internet advertising catches up to the science of online news delivery. Some news organizations might find sustenance in niche markets with programming such as Spanish-language or sports-intensive newscasts, but many will run into two big problems. First, their sites and those of their competitors will be similar, particularly in quasi-journalistic features such as events calendars, and movie and restaurant listings. The one or two most comprehensive and artfully presented services will probably satisfy the public and draw the advertisers. Second, although the Web sites might attract some new constituents, they will also pull people away from the parent organizations' newspaper or broadcasts, which will affect their revenues. "Profits" will be illusory if income is generated at the expense of another arm of the same entity.

One response to such difficulties will be a growing number of Web site partnerships among news organizations. A local television station and a newspaper might find it more economically sensible to combine rather than to compete online, even while keeping their respective on-air and on-paper efforts wholly separate. The systemic mechanics of such a relationship are complex but not overwhelming. The division of labor might, at least initially, follow lines of traditional expertise: television station personnel would be responsible for the site's video and audio content, while the newspaper's staff took the lead in text content. A combined editorial team would, presumably, decide what is to be covered and how it gets reported.

In Tampa, Florida, the *Tampa Tribune*, WFLA Television, and Tampa Bay Online have formed a combined news organization that is truly a joint venture. They coordinate coverage constantly, sharing a "superdesk" that directs assignments and tracks the progress of stories. Journalists' work product may be used on any or all of the three media outlets. A WFLA reporter might follow up a broadcast report by writing a *Tribune* story that incorporates material that was too long for the TV story, and Tampa Bay Online might feature video of entire interviews from which short sound bites were pulled for the original TV version.[9]

News organizations are also likely to rely on partnerships for non-news products, such as classified advertising. As noted in chapter 4, the paper classified section may soon become obsolete, but no newspaper can afford to lose such an important source of revenue. By combining their efforts, classified ad providers can offer the comprehensive and sophisticated listings that online consumers will expect. Regional and even national efforts along these lines are already operating; their scope makes them the advertising version of the news wire services.

Although much early focus has been on ads, in the future Web sites will largely depend on e-commerce for revenue, with media site proprietors getting a percentage of sales revenues generated from their sites. These transaction fees, according to Forrester Research, will provide media Web sites with $25 billion in revenue by 2003, while ads produce $17 billion and subscriptions $5 billion.[10] Traditional ads run on a fixed-rate basis, but the transaction fee system creates a tighter economic tie to the advertiser. This arrangement on the Internet, along with the specifically underwritten material that is becoming more common online, will test the independence and ethical resolve of news organizations.

Driving news and non-news partnerships will be an economic imperative based on evolving audience expectations. Just as the television viewer's eye has become accustomed to first-class production values in on-air presentations, so too are Web users coming to expect aesthetically appealing and easy-to-use online services. Given the exponential increases in Internet users and Web site providers, competition will be commensurately explosive. Going it alone might not be feasible except for a very few giants.

As with any product, pricing will be a big factor in determining market share. As the *Slate* magazine example cited earlier illustrates, advertising revenue alone may prove adequate to fund Web sites, much as it does broadcast television and radio. But the prospect of making money directly from consumers is still enticing. One approach is to offer free and premium services on the same site. Enough would be offered free to attract visitors and so satisfy advertisers, but some news material would be withheld for those with password access for which they pay a monthly or yearly fee. Some news analysis, databanks, and interactive features might be reserved for these paying customers. Even a clublike elitism may become a selling point, offering different levels of "membership" for the most serious news consumers. (Advertisers might be intrigued by this segmentation, which would allow more precisely targeted ad messages.) Some news organizations are trying this and will probably experiment with it for a while to determine what kind of fee structure the Internet-user market will sustain.

At the national level, a number of news organizations have been converging in ways that would have been considered unseemly just a few years ago. The *Washington Post* and *Newsweek* (both owned by the Washington Post Company) are sharing news content with NBC and MSNBC. The *New York Times* and ABC worked together on coverage of the 2000 political campaigns. The *Wall Street Journal* cooperates with CNBC, which is NBC's financial news cable channel.

This means that some *Post* stories, for example, will appear on MSNBC.com. The *Post* in turn gets access to NBC video for washingtonpost.com and could even use NBC stories in the paper. The network and the newspaper could try some joint reportorial ventures. The *Times* gets into the TV business by producing segments for *20/20* and *Good Morning America*.[11]

It's not that any of these news giants is incapable of doing its own work, but each wants to tap into still larger audience pools. MSNBC has the most popular news Web site, with more than 6.6 million monthly visitors by the end of 1999, while the *Post* had the sixth most popular news site, with about 1.6 million monthly visitors. Each might be able to steer some visitors to the partner's site. Expanded traffic means higher ad revenues.

Commercially, such partnerships make sense. Ethically, some questions arise. NBC is owned by General Electric. Microsoft is a partner in MSNBC. Both corporate titans are the subjects of lots of controversy and news coverage. In the *Post* newsroom, there were concerns not that the newspaper's coverage would be affected but that the public might *think* it was. Perception is important.[12]

After a while, multimedia teams will be common, and the resulting corporate entanglements may make the public even more cynical about the integrity of the news business. That is a natural response, and it is something journalists should keep in mind if they want their work to be taken seriously.

In addition to real or perceived conflicts of interest, joint ventures nationally and locally work against the diversity of news voices. Cooperation will produce homogeneity, which can cheat the public. Independent, competitive news gathering might produce better journalism than may emerge from economics-driven partnerships.

These issues and many others will be part of the media convergence that will gain momentum during the next few years, a process that will dramatically change the news business. For news organizations, a primary task will be to maintain ethical as well as financial equilibrium as the ground on which journalism stands trembles and shifts.

6

THE ETHICS MINEFIELD

For those who like to have specific dates to mark historic transitions, February 28, 1997, is worth remembering. One writer hailed it as "a kind of journalistic Bastille Day. Newspapers were liberated from the time constraints of printing press production, empowered to break news instantly."[1]

The event was the publication of a *Dallas Morning News* story about Oklahoma City bombing defendant Timothy McVeigh confessing to his lawyers that he had indeed set off the bomb that killed 168 people. What made this story particularly significant was not what it said but how it was delivered—on the paper's Web site seven hours before the regular edition was printed.

The story was immediately caught up in controversy about whether the *Morning News* had behaved ethically in revealing information that could prejudice the jury pool and impede McVeigh's chances of receiving a fair trial. That issue was debated angrily for a while, with McVeigh's attorneys charging improper behavior by *Morning News* reporters and the paper defending its news gathering. Eventually that dispute evaporated, leaving the Internet issue as the focus of attention. Writing in the *Columbia Journalism Review*, Christopher Hanson said that "this was apparently the first time a major newspaper had used the Web page to uncork such a huge, explosive story." Until recently, noted Hanson, newspapers "had avoided breaking stories on-line to avoid scooping themselves." That concern, he said, may be outweighed by several advantages: "to ensure getting credit for a perishable exclusive and to have global impact even if one's publication is regional."[2]

Morning News editor Ralph Langer said that the paper merely "did what CNN does. When the story was finished, we went with it."[3] According to media critic Jon Katz, "It's a long overdue recognition on the part of newspapers that if they want to stay in the breaking-news business, they need to use elec-tronic media to do it. They can't just come out once a day and be competitive."[4]

In this instance, the *Morning News* achieved its purpose: by first presenting the story online, it beat the competition and re-ceived wider and more immediate recognition for the scoop than would have been the case had the report just been pre-sented in the regular print editions. On the surface, this seems a straightforward matter of merely accelerating delivery of a story. But in a broader context, important ethical issues arise. Empha-sis on speed is an integral part of the news business, but for most newspaper journalists, the news cycle has been a daylong pro-cess, with a rhythm of reporting, fact-checking, and editing geared to meeting a firmly established deadline for producing the next edition of the paper. Using the Web site, however, re-quires a significant alteration of this newsroom culture. The deadline is always *now*. When Langer compared the delivery of the McVeigh story to CNN's procedures, he was implicitly not-ing this change.

This is not a minor adjustment. It demands new, systemic procedures to ensure the integrity of the news product. The re-sponsibilities of print news organizations in making this kind of change include establishing an enhanced array of editing capa-bilities to ensure that accuracy and context are not lost in the rush to be fast and faster. Ted Koppel said of this issue, "If we are moving into an era in which reporters are pressured to get it online before we have a chance to check and edit the material—if speed is the main criterion of putting something on line—then I think that's dangerous."[5]

Even among the Internet's biggest fans, few would contend that a journalistic utopia is in the offing. As evidence of online journalism's frailties, the new medium already features an inviting villain: Matt Drudge.

Casting himself as a latter-day Walter Winchell, Drudge has used the Internet to disseminate information, which he pointedly says is not the same as practicing traditional journalism. Getting started on his own and with almost no money, just a computer in a small apartment, Drudge offered a tiny audience items that he retrieved from trash cans at the Hollywood CBS studio where he worked. Gossip will always find an audience, and Drudge's following grew. He charges no fee to access his Web site, and in addition to his own tidbits provides links to news organizations and the work of individual journalists. Unconstrained by the practices of journalism, he presents entertaining, if sometimes nasty and not always accurate, stories. He writes about people while only occasionally seeking comment from them. If a rumor is "out there," floating along the edges of the political or media mainstream, he deems it publishable.

While a reporter or news organization is carefully verifying a story, Drudge may pounce. For him, absolute truth matters less than absolute speed. He has his own sources within the news business, and he constantly scans news Web sites to find out what news organizations around the world will be presenting when they next go to press or go on the air. Then he blithely scoops them. This is the inherent danger in using the Web to offer previews of coming attractions. It might seem to be a good way to advertise stories, but a pirate such as Drudge may kidnap the previews and be the first to get them to the public.

Coverage of the 1998 White House sex scandal was a testing

ground for Drudge, as it was for Internet journalism. This medium has an egalitarian appeal as the latest version of the basement printing press on which anyone has the right to propound his or her views and disseminate them as he or she chooses. The great difference, of course, between the basement printing press and the Internet is reach. Matt Drudge can sit in his apartment, crank out his *Drudge Report,* and instantly make it available to millions. His expenses are negligible, his reach enormous.

Drudge is proudly cavalier about fact-checking, which has earned him the disdain of mainstream journalists, but many of them still read him for entertainment and as a source of lurid tips. He has become a minor celebrity, a figure both treacherous and comic, often referred to in mocking terms.

For the journalists whose stories Drudge scoops, he is not to be lightly dismissed. In 1998, Michael Isikoff of *Newsweek* found that the *Drudge Report* was carrying parts of a story he was working on about Kathleen Willey, who accused President Clinton of sexual misconduct. The story had not yet appeared in *Newsweek* because it was not judged ready for publication, a fact that apparently did not bother Drudge. Isikoff said, "He's rifling through raw reporting like raw FBI files, and disseminating it. He doesn't conform to any journalistic standard. This is not harmless fun; it's reckless and ought to be condemned. . . . It's hard to do real reporting in an atmosphere that's been polluted like this."[6]

More importantly, Drudge has affected the rules of news delivery. He can take a story that has been judged by a news organization as not yet ready for publication, shine his own spotlight on it, and force it onto the public news agenda. His most famous piracy was the initial *Newsweek* story by Isikoff about Monica Lewinsky's relationship with Bill Clinton. The magazine was not ready to publish, but when a *Newsweek* source told Drudge the gist of the story, he had no such reluctance. He told the world that *Newsweek* was sitting on the story. It was now "out there" enough to find a home on quasi-news venues, such as Rush Limbaugh's radio talk show and Jay Leno's *Tonight Show* monologue. Once the huge audiences of these and similar programs learn about a story, many in the mainstream media rush to catch up.

Some journalists, however, have not abandoned restraint. Ann McDaniel, *Newsweek*'s managing editor and Washington bureau chief, anticipated being scooped on the Lewinsky story:

> When we didn't publish Monica the first weekend, we knew there was no chance that in the seven days that followed somebody would not break the story. But it did not meet our standards and we chose not to publish. It was an extraordinarily difficult decision. We like to be first. But we like more to be accurate. . . . We weren't going to violate our standards just to get out there with it.[7]

In addition to raiding other journalists' work, Drudge presents his own "world exclusives" that he hammers together from leaks and leftovers. When he is wrong, he is unrepentant. Asked about not checking out a story that proved incorrect, he simply said, "It's the nature of what I do—I move quickly."[8]

That cavalier attitude about the truth can infect the larger news-gathering process. News on the Internet becomes a stimulus to the rest of the news business. Print, broadcast, and cable converge with Web news carriers in the effort to match whatever the front-runner is offering. There is nothing new about journalists trying to best someone else's scoop, but when the "someone else" is Drudge and the scoop is gossip, not verified news, journalistic standards may be knocked askew. *Washington Post* media critic Howard Kurtz has noted that "gossip is naughty, delicious, unverified—all the things that mainstream journalism is not."[9] *Newsweek*'s Isikoff, whose Willey and Lewinsky stories Drudge preempted, offers a harsher appraisal of Drudge:

He's a menace to honest, responsible journalism. He's clearly willing to go with anything, whether he's got any legitimate sourcing, anything approaching legitimate verification. He doesn't conform to any journalistic standard or convention that I'm aware of. And to the extent that he's read and people believe what they read, he's dangerous.[10]

Drudge sees himself as an "information anarchist," doing his work in a way that "makes me editor of the entire media world."[11] He says: "Clearly there is a hunger for unedited information. . . . We have entered an era vibrating with the din of small voices. Every citizen can be a reporter, can take on the powers that be."[12] Drudge points out that everyone using the Internet has direct access to the news wires and other sources that previously were available only to newsroom denizens. Every day, editors take this mountain of information and shape it into a relatively small, tightly packed mound of news. Now, says Drudge, "with a modem, anyone can follow the world and report on the world—no middle man, no big brother."[13]

There will be no editors in the Internet world, says Drudge, as individuals publish online whatever they choose. "What is civilization going to do," he asks, "with the ability of one citizen—without advertisers, without an editor" to reach millions? "The conscience," he says, "is going to be the only thing between us and communication in the future."[14]

The tension between Drudge and mainstream journalism is palpable. Drudge proudly says, "I am not a professional journalist."[15] Or, when he is feeling more prickly, "Screw journalism! The whole thing's a fraud anyway!"[16] Drudge's career benefits from fortuitous timing. His antipress attitude probably wins him applause from a scandal-weary public ready to believe the worst of the news business. He certainly has found an audience. He reported 115 million visits to his site during 1998, up from 31 million in 1997. The busiest day in 1998 was September 10, in the midst of the White House scandal, with 1,162,553 visits. By mid-2000, he was reporting an average of more than a million daily visits.

Drudge's success is a symbol of change and a warning about the difficulty of preserving standards. Beyond the Drudge example, perhaps the most important and most difficult adjustment that online journalism requires is systemic adaptation to the allure of cyberspeed news delivery. Solid news judgment is most threatened by the emphasis on speed. Instant availability of a story can come to be regarded as more important than its relevance. Disseminating it quickly may be rated more highly than confirming its accuracy.

Beyond Drudge's behavior, those interested in the ethics of the news business are more concerned about the way mainstream journalists themselves use the Internet. On February 4, 1998, a *Wall Street Journal* reporter called the White House for comment about the newspaper's information that a White House steward had told a federal grand jury that he had seen President Clinton and Monica Lewinsky alone together in the president's study. White House spokesman Joe Lockhart told the reporter he would have to check, but moments later the reporter told him that the story had just been posted on the *Journal*'s Web site. The story, which cited unnamed sources, also was quickly put on the *Journal*'s wire service, and the paper's Washington bureau chief talked about it on cable news channel CNBC. Within ninety minutes, the steward's lawyer issued a statement calling the *Journal*'s story "absolutely false and irresponsible." The paper, while standing by the basic information in the story, later changed its report to say that the steward had reported his observation to "Secret Service personnel," not the grand jury.[17] That is a significant difference.

Washington Post media critic Howard Kurtz wrote that this case illustrated "the increasing velocity of the news cycle" and noted that one of the *Journal* reporters had explained the rush by saying, "We heard footsteps from at least one other news organization and just didn't think it was going to hold in this crazy cycle we're in."[18]

The Internet itself and its "crazy cycle" should not be blamed for lapses such as the one in the *Journal* case. Jack Shafer of the online magazine *Slate* said that "critics seem to think the Internet has an especially demonic power to distort. . . . But technology is neutral. It makes as much sense to blame modems and the Internet for distorting the spread of news as it does to blame telephones."[19]

Nevertheless, the Internet's rapid delivery is so appealing that it could foster ethical anarchy unless news purveyors pay close attention to the responsibilities that accompany speed. Tom Rosenstiel, director of the Project for Excellence in Journalism, wrote, "At a minimum, newspaper organizations will begin to make more mistakes—if only on their Web sites. But that alone will affect the public's perception of them. More mistakes equal less public trust."[20]

This issue is made more complicated by the interactive nature of news Web sites. That has produced different rules governing the accuracy of different categories of material that appear on the sites. A regular story on a newspaper's site will, presumably, conform to the newspaper's standards of accuracy and fairness. But when readers respond with their own comments that are posted on the site's message board or chat room, those comments might not meet those same standards. Steven Brill, publisher of the media analysis magazine *Brill's Content*, said of this, "I still think we are responsible in the sense that I reserve the right to edit stuff that is in bad taste or grossly unfair to people—within the parameters that the bulletin board is a place for people to discuss all kinds of opinion."[21]

The interactive capability of the Internet news site is one of its great advantages, but interactivity creates its own challenges. If the news organization places its imprimatur on the site, it apparently assumes that readers will distinguish between the journalist-generated and audience-generated material and will appreciate the different rules that apply to each. That may be a lot to ask of a public that is not familiar with the fine points of journalistic protocol.

The problem in cases such as the *Wall Street Journal* example involves more than the nuances of news operations. It represents a collapse of process: at least some of the fact-checking accompanied or followed, rather than preceded, posting of the story. This was not an isolated instance. Some news organizations have even formally introduced a "fudge factor" that allows posting preliminary information on the Web site without full confirmation. Readers are told that this is just the first take of the story and that they should return to the site for later developments. Some journalists don't like this approach, but its defenders say that the public has come to expect a steady diet of timely news. Thus an unconfirmed report is presented, with the caveat that it will be checked further by the news organization.[22]

A kind of temporal disorientation seems to take hold in such cases and has the potential to infect much of online journalism. To correct this, newsroom procedures should be firmly defined to reinstate the proper priorities. The old wire service maxim, "Get it first, but first get it right," may seem quaintly archaic, but it still makes a lot of sense.

At the heart of this transformation in journalism is the culture of most newsrooms, which is grounded in the news cycle. Depending on their frequency of publication (on paper or electronically), the process of gathering, evaluating, verifying, and then reporting the news is calibrated according to a schedule. Remove that temporal framework and intellectual anarchy gains a foothold in the newsroom. Journalist James Naughton wrote that "the digital age does not respect contemplation. . . . Now there are no cycles, only Now."[23]

To argue that traditional cycles must be maintained is like

trying to drive back the incoming tide. Instantaneous news, for good or ill (or both), is here. Many variations of the *Dallas Morning News* and *Wall Street Journal* cases lie ahead. To sustain the integrity of journalism in whatever form it takes, the news business must redesign its practices, beginning with a renewed commitment to the profession's ethics.

THE ETHICS OF CONVERGENCE

Journalism ethics is the subject of persistent debate, and deservedly so, given the pervasiveness and influence of the news media. But a precise definition of "ethical" remains elusive, as does an understanding of what new ethical issues are presented by the rise of "new media," such as Web-delivered journalism.

Uncertainty may be inescapable, but the ethical framework of the news business must be expanded as the newest forms of journalism are being constructed. Merely saying "journalism is journalism and ethics is ethics" is not good enough. Although fundamental principles of ethical journalism apply to new media as well as old, they must be adapted to technology-driven changes in the profession. One useful function of convergence is that it may push those concerned about journalism to evaluate the state of news ethics and upgrade them where appropriate.

Individually and collectively, journalists are grappling with online ethics in a more comprehensive, systematic way and not just on a case-by-case basis. Writing in the *American Journalism Review*, online journalist Barb Palser identified some ethics topics that news organizations should address:[24]

- Creating and posting a privacy policy.
- Having standards for sites linked to the home news site.
- Providing a disclaimer or warning before a page that site visitors may find offensive.

- Maintaining reasonable visual distinction between ads and editorial content.
- Presenting corrections in ways most likely to undo the damage that the original error may have caused.
- Respecting copyrighted material and acknowledging items from other sites.
- Posting guidelines for chat rooms or other pages for visitors' comments.

Most of these issues are not far removed from concerns that have long been issues in pre-Internet news. Particularly because of the perceived closeness that the Web fosters between news provider and news consumer, these matters have taken on new significance in the online delivery of information. The topics Palser itemizes are similar to issues addressed in the founding principles of the Online News Association, which was established by journalists who recognized that a new medium requires a new look at professional ethics. Similarly, the *Online Journalism Review*, published at the University of Southern California, often focuses on ethical issues of principal interest to online newspeople.

These organized efforts reflect the concerns of many of the individual journalists who create the online news product. Their thinking in some ways mirrors that of the radio and television journalists who provide real-time news. They too recognize that technological advances—particularly in terms of speedy news delivery—require renewed commitment to ethics and creative thinking about responsibilities to the public and to their own profession.

One of the general concerns is the question of responsibility for content. The Internet is something of an intellectual Wild West: it offers exciting opportunity but also potentially harmful disorder. Needed now is a benign sheriff in the form of ethics guidelines that let the freedoms of the Web flourish but also prevent Web journalism from betraying the public's trust.

As Matt Drudge's operating style illustrates, delivering news to the public on the Internet can be done without passing through the internal newsroom checkpoints that are part of traditional journalism. Drudge (and others) would presumably contend that this is not necessarily bad because those checkpoints too often block information that the public has a right and need to know. That may be a valid argument in some cases, but the checkpoints also can foster accuracy and fairness, values that journalistic gunslingers such as Drudge sometimes treat lightly.

There is room for all kinds of reporting on the Internet, but the medium's openness can be easily abused. This was evident in September 1997 when a photograph disseminated on the Web purported to show the body of Princess Diana in her wrecked automobile in Paris. The photograph showed firefighters at the scene of a car accident, but their uniforms were not those of the Paris fire brigades and their truck was marked with an emergency phone number that could not have been used in France. Despite these flaws, the picture was published on the front page of a French newspaper and was distributed by an Italian news agency. The original online source of the photo was an American anticensorship group, which had never claimed the image was real.[25] Phony pictures are nothing new, but their speedy, broad dissemination via the Internet is. For those members of the public who get information directly off the Web, this open access forgoes the checking an editor could provide. For news organizations, this should be a cautionary tale. When sources of information are not known, extra care should be part of decisions about whether to publish.

Not all Web-related ethical problems can be attributed to Matt Drudge or groups on the journalistic fringe. Even the most venerable news organizations want profits promptly from their online products, and the resulting pressure on editors and reporters can lead to corner cutting in the preparation of news stories. Mainstream news organizations operating in this way compound the problems created by the less responsible news providers. As new-media expert J. D. Lasica has noted, "The public needs reputable news outlets to adhere to their core values of accuracy, credibility and balance to give stories . . . context and perspective, a role that other media have forfeited."[26] Reassertion of these core values might ensure a degree of balance in the sometimes dizzying array of news items provided by online sources.

In addition to offering that steadiness, news organizations must devise ethical standards for new components of their business, such as the use of links. Some news organizations say that links are provided as a service to readers, with no guarantees about veracity. Is this good enough? Alternatively, a news organization might use an on-screen disclaimer to announce that the site visitor is "leaving the premises" when clicking to go to a link. But is even that good enough? According to Bob Steele of the Poynter Institute,

> We cannot just say "Buyer beware." That alone does not mitigate against the harm that can come from tainted information. . . . I've never liked the word "disclaimer." It means, "I do not claim responsibility." I don't believe that's an appropriate position for a news organization to take.[27]

Yet another possible policy for links is to withhold them from individuals or organizations that espouse violence, racism, or other such behavior. That sounds good, but at what point in the exclusion process does censorship begin? Chat rooms may create similar problems. If a news organization provides a chat room on its site, what responsibility, if any, does it have for the content of the chat? Again, good intentions about propriety can slide into censorship.

These quandaries are products of the unrestrained character of Internet communication. Cyberjournalism by its very nature defies rules. That makes online ethics a frustratingly slippery topic. Trying to come up with guidelines for Web-based journalism can seem like trying to grab a wet bar of soap.

Real-time issues are just part of this. Online news products face demands that have much in common with the ethical tasks wire services have been dealing with for many years. The wire services have proved that speed and responsibility need not be mutually exclusive. Complicating matters, however, is the growing crowd. So many news organizations are, in one form or another, delivering real-time journalism that the intensity of competition sometimes overshadows concerns about professional responsibility. One way to respond to this is by assertively addressing ethics issues, such as by posting ethics policies. *TheStreet.com*, an online-only financial news publication, posts its "conflicts and disclosure policy" on its site. It tells readers that editorial staff members may not hold positions in individual stocks. They may own mutual fund shares, but if writing about a fund in which they hold shares, a disclosure will be made. The publication's business staff, members of its board, and even outside columnists are governed by in-house rules. The page further lists *TheStreet.com*'s investors, underwriters, and distributors. This is probably more information than most people will want to know, but the fact that there is a clearly defined ethics policy may in itself reassure visitors to the site.

Corrections policy is also particularly important for online news providers. The easiest way to fix a mistake is simply to erase it and replace it with the correct information. That is a temptation unique to electronic publication, since there is no "original" version in the print or video archives. Unless someone saved the early version or printed out a copy of the uncorrected material, there is no evidence that anything was ever wrong. This is fine for readers who come to the site after the correction has been made. But failure to post a formal notice of correction implies that there was never an error, and that is less than honest.

The ethics of Internet journalism will be shaped partly by the evolving body of law related to this area of public communication. Basic rules, such as those regarding libel, will apply to Web news but will have to be tailored to meet new media exigencies. The ranks of journalists will certainly grow as anyone who wants to create a "news" Web site may do so and disseminate material globally with a click of the mouse. The First Amendment contains no definition of "journalist" and its protections will, presumably, continue to extend to those who reasonably claim to be part of the trade.

One of the most contentious matters in the early days of Web news is defining who is responsible for what appears online. The writer of the material is responsible, but is the online service as well? When Matt Drudge was sued by White House aide Sidney Blumenthal for alleging—incorrectly—that Blumenthal had "a spousal abuse past," Blumenthal also sued America Online, which carries Drudge's *Drudge Report*. If AOL is a publisher, with control over editorial content, it might be liable. But if it is merely a common carrier or the equivalent of a newsstand, then it is not legally responsible for all its wares.[28] Initial court decisions indicate that the exercise of editorial discretion will be a crucial factor in determining liability.

There will also be legal questions about ownership of online property, and access restrictions that might be viewed as censorship. Guidelines about such matters will evolve in and out of court. With online journalism, as with other news media, the extent of intrusion by law will be determined partly by the rigorousness of ethical self-policing.

Even as the Internet develops, television continues to provide a dynamic testing ground for journalism ethics, with lessons applicable to other real-time media, whether they be broadcast, cable, or online.

An example of the always evolving process of gathering news was the April 1999 coverage of the shootings at Columbine High School in Littleton, Colorado. Live reports from the scene were gripping. The Denver-area television news teams did a superb job in terms of the mechanics of delivering the story to their audience. Veteran journalist Dean Rotbart spent the day of the shootings in the newsroom of CBS-owned Denver station KCNC and later presented his findings in the *Columbia Journalism Review*. He praised the station's efforts:

> Producers and reporters dug out this fluid and complex story in the best journalistic tradition, calling sources, knocking on doors, surfing the Internet to find Web sites that the shooters had set up. With amazing speed, the news team came up with important details, notably the identities of the two student gunmen. But the station didn't rush to air with its scoop until staff members could get double and triple confirmations, which took several hours.
>
> Nor did the station opt to show gore. KCNC editors had plenty of film to exploit had they wanted. In particular, cameramen captured one police SWAT team dragging two of the victims' bodies across the school's lawn—images that never once aired. In the heat of the story chase, newsroom editors talked about their responsibilities to decency and community values.[29]

But some questionable decisions were made even in the midst of this good-faith effort to provide a responsible news product. Rotbart reported that a KCNC crew had been allowed to set up on the roof of a residence near the school. Viewers could watch police snipers taking aim at the building and could see the faces of students trapped inside the school.[30]

This may be gripping television, but it illustrates a persistent problem that accompanies live reporting of this kind of event. There were televisions in the school, so it was conceivable that the gunmen were also watching this coverage, studying the police deployment and learning where students were hiding. If the shooters had seen this and acted on it, the tragedy of Columbine could have been exacerbated.

This kind of situation helped prompt the Radio and Television News Directors Foundation and Bob Steele of the Poynter Institute of Media Studies to suggest guidelines for covering hostage taking, police raids, terrorist acts, and other such crises. The first of the sixteen guidelines is, "Always assume that the hostage taker, gunman, or terrorist has access to the reporting." Among their other recommendations are the following:

- Avoid describing with words or showing with still photography and video any information that could divulge the tactics or positions of SWAT team members.
- Be forthright with viewers, listeners, or readers about why certain information is being withheld if security reasons are involved.
- Seriously weigh the benefits to the public of what information might be given out versus what potential harm that information might cause. This is especially important in live reporting of an ongoing situation.
- Keep news helicopters out of the area where the standoff is happening, as their noise can create communication problems for negotiators and their presence could scare a gunman to deadly action.[31]

These guidelines are helpful because they guide stations toward systematizing their approaches to covering this kind of crisis. If adopted by stations, these standards might inhibit some of the riskier coverage tactics.

The Columbine coverage was a good example of television journalists being responsive and trying to do a better job. That is the essence of ethics in any news medium. If those who do on-line news follow this same path, they will have a good chance to find their way through the ethics minefield.

7

SAILING THE UNCHARTED SEA

I n his book *The Lexus and the Olive Tree, New York Times* columnist Thomas Friedman wrote, "The Internet is going to be like
a huge vise that takes the globalization system . . . and keeps
tightening and tightening that system around everyone, in ways
that will only make the world smaller and smaller and faster and
faster with each passing day."[1] This tightening will enhance the
"global village" that Marshall McLuhan prophesied. It will affect news delivery and news consumption, raising expectations
about the speed and breadth of coverage and presenting complex challenges to those who want to provide that coverage re-
sponsibly.

No one should be surprised by the expanding demands that
the news business will face. The new media may differ from earlier media physically but not in content. A logical progression
links traditional journalism and this "new news." Likewise, in
terms of real-time coverage, there is a direct path from live radio
and television to real-time news delivery on the Web.

These paths are now headed toward convergence. How
long they prove to be will depend on two principal factors from
the public's standpoint: affordability and transparency. Consumers are enjoying a sharp decline in the cost of the hardware
needed to use the Internet. As prices decline, the numbers of
users will climb and socioeconomic barriers to Web access will

159

fall. The next generation of children will be computer literate and computer equipped. Widespread use of the Internet in schools is already creating a generation of Web users who see the Internet not as a strange new curiosity but an accepted tool of everyday life. (These schoolchildren may be too young to show up now in most surveys that measure Internet use, but they are certainly out there, in large and growing numbers.)

The easy comparison is to the rise of television during the 1950s, but there are important differences between watching television and using the Internet. Television sets vary in size and quality, but for the most part they are stationary objects within the household, like other pieces of furniture. The computer, however, is not so limited. Going beyond the familiar desktop assemblage, the new array of information appliances will make the computer a much more diverse and adaptable appliance than the television ever was. The transparency of Internet use will be enhanced as news consumers acquire the habit of tapping a few keys on a wireless telephone or other handy device to check the news on the Web. Speed of delivery of Web site material and ease of use—such as "turning the pages" of an online newspaper—will also improve steadily.

The comparison with television raises a cautionary point about Web use projections. Some people may prefer the more passive role of traditional television watching. Even when the Web is integrated with TV, the Internet user must exert some intellectual effort. There may be those—who knows how many—who are quite happy to watch Jerry Springer and sitcoms and not bother with anything more demanding. This "couch potato corollary" to the general theory of expanding Internet use will challenge the creativity of those who are trying to enhance the allure of Web sites.

Regardless of technological advances and audience curiosity, news organizations will find that the road to online affordability (and then profitability) is going to be bumpy. Deciding what information to provide and how to provide it will involve a trial-and-error process pushed along by competition. In 1999, Time Warner shut down its Pathfinder Web site, which was the shared home of *Time, Fortune, Entertainment Weekly,* and other publications. Time Warner decided instead to capitalize on its well-recognized individual brands and feature Time.com, Fortune.com, and so on.[2] The move reflects the parent company's response to Web users' desire for fast, convenient access to the particular sites. Also, Time Warner assumes that audience segmentation will facilitate marketing through the varied sites.

Time Warner will not be the only communications organization to rethink and restructure its Web presence. The next few years will see much research and trial-and-error testing of the marketplace as new media providers make sure their products match the interests of new media consumers.

New media will pass through a time of fierce competition marked by coming together and shaking out. Lots of online offerings will not survive: the market can sustain only so many. As with other businesses, the best-funded and most creatively managed efforts will rise to the top. New alliances will mark a significant restructuring of the news business, some between longtime competitors that find it both journalistically efficient and financially beneficial to undertake new joint media ventures. Also, corporations thought of as primarily non-news businesses, such as AOL and Microsoft, will increasingly be major players in Web-oriented journalistic enterprises.

Media mergers are another form of convergence. They create industry entities that engulf media properties like the giant protoplasm in a horror movie. The mergers may lead to increased profits but diminished diversity of journalistic enterprises. The Tribune–Times Mirror merger in 2000 made financial sense, but it raised further fears about the trend toward a narrow perspective on deciding what is news. Coalescing around a few leaders might also occur among online news ventures, with similar muting of independent voices.

While this sorting out is under way, the people doing new media journalism will have plenty of issues to address, particularly about ethics. The "Drudge effect"—shoot-from-the-hip sensationalism—will give online journalism a bad name if the public perceives it to be a dominant characteristic of this medium. The best way for responsible journalists to deal with the Matt Drudges (imitators of the original are sure to appear) is to isolate them by delivering a consistently fair and accurate online news product.

Talking about fairness and accuracy is easy; achieving it is more difficult, particularly given the temptations that online delivery creates for news organizations. Some of the investments in media enterprises go to develop technology and gimmicks, not basic journalism. In journalism, broadband delivery will mean little without broad-based news gathering. The notion that the public demands high-speed news is one of those self-perpetuating axioms that should be challenged. Reasserting the primacy of accuracy and taste will not drive the audience away.

A high-quality product, even if delivered deliberately rather than instantaneously, might be welcomed by an audience grown tired of relentless emphasis on real-time news. Commitment to quality must be industry-wide if it is to be meaningful. Nobility is endangered when left to stand alone. Once the number of news organizations and individual journalists willing to reaffirm editorial responsibility reaches a critical mass, news consumers' expectations might change as well. Tabloid-style news will always have a following, but it need not pollute mainstream journalism. Online offerings' particular susceptibility to speed-driven news judgments should be addressed early on as news organizations build their online entities. Failure to do so may allow the "Drudge effect" to gain a more lasting foothold.

Just as the online news providers have journalistic vulnerabilities, so too do they have strengths. Interactivity, if used creatively, might redefine the relationship between news provider and news consumer. For example, the *Brill's Content* Web site includes a "media complaint" message board on which site visitors may post their gripes and receive comments and responses. By bringing public concerns into public view, this kind of mechanism may improve the accountability of news organizations and may increase news consumers' faith in the integrity of those organizations.

When journalists create participatory mechanisms such as message boards and chat rooms, they implicitly promise to increase their responsiveness to those who use them. The great potential of interactivity will never be fulfilled unless a good-faith effort is made by all parties to communicate in the truest sense of the word. That means that a "media complaint" board should not be viewed by news professionals as merely a place for the public to blow off steam. For one thing, many of the public's complaints about the news media are well founded. Journalists should set aside their delusions of perfection, recognize they are not flawless, and address public concerns with the seriousness that they merit.

That in itself will require a change in the journalistic culture, which tends to dismiss people with complaints as "nut cases" to be dealt with as expeditiously as possible. Journalists who retain that view will be courting trouble, largely because exchanges in many of the new media forums will not be private one-to-one communication but rather will be accessible by a larger audience. The openness that many journalists insist is so important in covering government and other institutions is becoming a more significant issue within the news business itself because of the visibility of process that online communication allows.

As public attitudes about online journalism evolve, news professionals themselves have changing feelings about the new media. A 1999 survey by Middleberg and Associates of newspaper and magazine managing editors and business editors found that 73 percent reported going online at least once a day, compared to 48 percent in 1998 and 17 percent in 1994. Respondents who said that they never or almost never went online dropped from 37 percent in 1994 to 1 percent in 1999. Also, more than 50 percent of the respondents said they used e-mail to communicate with readers.[3]

A 1999 report by the Pew Research Center for the People and the Press noted a significant difference in attitudes between those who do online news and traditional practitioners. Approximately half of the mainstream news organization journalists surveyed for the report said that the emergence of the Internet has made journalism better, whereas four out of five online journalists feel that way. The journalists' age is also a factor: 70 percent of those thirty-four or younger say the Internet has improved the news business, an opinion shared by 53 percent of those between thirty-five and fifty-four and 40 percent of those fifty-five or older. (These findings relate largely to the use of the Net as an information-gathering tool).[4]

Another topic that elicits distinctly different opinions concerns the public's ability to use the Internet for direct access to the news, bypassing news organizations. Seventy-four percent of the online journalists think this is a positive effect of the Internet, but fewer than half of traditional media journalists agree.[5]

An even more substantive difference can be seen in the attitudes about the tone and substance of news. Fewer online journalists think that "always remaining neutral" and "avoiding use of first person" are core principles of journalism. The online journalists also are more likely than their mainstream colleagues to believe that "providing an interpretation" of the news is a core principle.[6]

These differences reflect a generational shift that is accompanying the expansion of the news business to accommodate online journalism. The new attitudes may foreshadow a permanent change in the philosophy of journalism, or they may be a temporary phenomenon that will swing back toward traditional standards as the new media mature. However transient these attitudes may be, they deserve attention because they are likely to affect news content, at least for the foreseeable future.

They also have ramifications for journalism education, which will shape the standards that the next generation of journalists will bring to a profession in which new media play an ever larger role. Increasingly in vogue is "cross-training" journalism students to ensure multimedia proficiency. Walls between print, broadcast, and online journalism are coming down in schools just as they are in the profession. The task for journalism educators, as for working journalists, is to avoid getting too caught up in the technological aspects of the new news and shortchanging the fundamentals of professional responsibility.

An NBC job posting in spring 2000 for an "interactive content developer" offers an indication of the convergence-oriented world these new journalists will enter:

> The job entails understanding how text, audio, and video are combined and used to create a compelling online product. The candidate should have some knowledge of content acquisition, channel development, and local Web site production. We are looking for someone who has a strong sense of changing deadlines and workflow throughout the day. The successful candidate will also possess excellent knowledge of the Internet and an appreciation of graphic images and design and how they work together to make Web pages richer. . . . Must have some familiarity with PhotoShop, Premiere, and Sound Forge and have experience in JAVA, HTML, and JavaScript programming languages.

That's a long way from a job that Tom Brokaw would have applied for.

As the content of the new media evolves, patterns of news

consumption will be changing too. The Internet provides various modes of news delivery, such as a crawl of headlines across the bottom of the computer screen and other constant reminders of what is going on in the world. Tracking the use of this and other such services might allow a census of hard-core new media news junkies. Who are these people who must have news and more news? A longer-term question will be to determine what effect this increased availability of information has on news consumption. Will the constant presence produce an addiction to news or will people find ubiquitous journalism annoying? Also, how will people use all this news? Will more news mean greater voter participation or other civic involvement?

The mere availability of more news does not ensure that it will be welcomed, nor does it mean that the news audience will expand. That remains one of the great mysteries of online news—just how much of it is wanted and how many people want it? The answers to such questions will do much to define the news content and business structure of online journalism. As those answers take shape, there will be plenty of temptations to use electronic gimmickry to try to hook consumers. That approach has two intrinsic flaws. First, it is likely to exacerbate the problems related to premature reporting because providing "up-to-the-second" bulletins will probably be a key selling point for screen crawls, "news alerts," and other such packaging. Second, it may produce a misleading estimate of long-term audience size because the charms of the gimmicks might prove only temporary.

These matters become more complex when the news consumers themselves determine at least some of the content they will receive. "Customized news" is attractive because it highlights interactivity and gives audience members the feeling that they, rather than the faceless "media," are making decisions about which news topics are important.

Turning over decisions about newsworthiness to news consumers has populist appeal, but tunnel vision may result. One of the duties of journalists is to present even unpleasant and complex information if they decide that the public needs to know about it. There may be something patronizing about this, but it remains a duty of responsible journalism.

When offering Web site visitors the "customized news" list of topics from which they might select, few might choose Central Africa, for example. But if a devastating famine strikes that region, the public should be told about it. Another example: in 1998, how many news consumers would have put Kosovo on their lists? It was a horrifying story and, at least initially, difficult to understand. But, as it turned out, it was also exceptionally important.

Preselecting news topics inevitably means screening out stories. This approach may let parochialism flourish and may constrain the growth of knowledge. Maybe the "one size fits all" approach to news is no longer commercially viable, but if news organizations abdicate from their intellectual and moral leadership roles, they would be paying a high price for perhaps getting a larger audience.

Of course, it may turn out that the interactive capabilities of online news are overrated in terms of news consumers' interest in them. A public that has grown up ingesting words and images from the broadcast media might not want to commit the time or energy to this kind of journalism. Younger news consumers—those who are growing up with the computer and the Internet as standard tools of everyday life—will provide the first testing ground for active versus passive news products. As Web news develops, news organizations will need to decide how much money and effort they want to devote to creating a news product that is more than just a warmed-over version of what other media offer. Beyond real-time and interactive features, news on the Web can provide rich context by presenting much background and explanation. How well this is done will be the key to the qualitative success or failure of this news medium.

Because Web news is such a new medium, its long-term effect on the news business is still difficult to predict. But a Pew Research Center study released in June 2000 reported that the number of people getting news online is growing, and a growing proportion of those people are using other news sources less frequently. Whether that is a blip or evidence of a trend will become clear before long.

Some years will pass as patterns of news consumption evolve. In the meantime, broadcast and cable news organizations have an obligation to improve their standards and content, regardless of what they think the future will bring. In journalism as in other professions, advances in technology can easily outstrip progress in ethics. Television's sometimes rocky experiences in live coverage, especially of crises, should be put to good use in designing guidelines for live reporting on the Web. The bulletin-delivery service that is already a principal feature of some Internet news services is especially susceptible to errors in fact and in judgment.

The progression from broadcast to cable to Web is leading to a convergence of not only technologies but also the core principles of a profession. As with all the other aspects of Web-based news providers, the new media will be (or at least should be) influenced by the experiences of what may come to be called "the established media" and then perhaps "old media." Ethical codes, for instance, need not be constructed from scratch. Their specifics will, in some ways, differ from those of other media, but these differences will be far less significant than the similarities in fundamental responsibilities to the public and to journalism as a profession. Convergence may turn out to be far less traumatic than some pessimists would have the public (and journalists themselves) believe.

That is not to understate the profound changes that Web

news will bring about. The increased accessibility of information is, in itself, revolutionary. Anyone able to connect to the Internet has the world's news at his or her disposal, and any efforts to impede this access will prove decreasingly successful as the new media's pervasiveness and technological sophistication increase. This is not merely a matter of reading uncensored text. Broadcasters are already using the Internet to subvert efforts to block their work. In 1996, the Serbian government began jamming the signal of Belgrade radio B92 when the station carried reports about protests against Slobodan Milosevic's regime. The station, however, sent RealAudio versions of its broadcasts to its Web site on a Dutch service provider, so Internet users within Yugoslavia and elsewhere could listen to B92's coverage on the Web. Radio Free Europe also picked up the station's material from the Net and broadcast it back into Serbia, bypassing Milosevic's censors.[7] This showcases a powerful facet of convergence and shows how the Web can be a valuable instrument of freedom.

For all the talk about the duties of new media journalists, there also are clear responsibilities for the citizen in the new media era. Not everyone need become a news fanatic, but all people with access to the Internet should use the newly deepened reservoir of news to raise their level of knowledge about events in community, nation, and world. On election day, no one with Internet access will be able to plead a shortage of information about candidates and issues as an excuse for not voting. As many campaigns from top to bottom of the ballot in 2000 illustrated, the Internet offers not only unprecedented amounts of information, but also—in many races—the opportunity for interactive communication among politicians, journalists, and voters. Online voting, which some states experimented with in the 2000 elections, will become much more common. (That may produce an interesting debate about just how easy voting should be. If ballots can be cast with the click of a mouse, participation may increase, but how knowledgeable will those new participants be?) News consumers also have a responsibility to learn about online news issues, such as those related to speed of news delivery and the quality information sources that are found on the Web. The public can do much to push the news business toward higher standards.

As important as the public's obligations are, they do not diminish the responsibilities of the news media in the real-time world. The women and men of the news business must use the new media to achieve the traditional goals of journalism—to provide, fairly and accurately, the information the public wants and needs to know. The speed and impact of real-time news should complement, not dominate, that mission.

The technology of communication may change, but the task for news professionals is what it has always been: to act in good faith, doing journalism well and passionately.

NOTES

CHAPTER 1

1. Pew Research Center for the People and the Press, "The Internet News Audience Goes Ordinary," news release, January 14, 1999, 14.

2. Andrew Kohut, "Internet Users Are on the Rise, but Public Affairs Interest Isn't," *Columbia Journalism Review*, January-February 2000, 68.

3. Pew Research Center for the People and the Press, "Internet News Takes Off," news release, June 8, 1998, 12.

4. Pew Center, "Internet News Takes Off," 12.

5. Pew Center, "Internet News Takes Off," 3.

6. Pew Center for the People and the Press, "Stock Market Down, New Media Up," news release, November 9, 1997.

7. Peter Burrows, "Cheap PCs," *BusinessWeek*, March 23, 1998, 28–29.

8. Claude Moisy, "Myths of the Global Information Village," *Foreign Policy* 107 (Summer 1997): 80.

9. Mark Hall, "One-to-One Politics in Cyberspace," *Media Studies Journal*, Winter 1997, 102.

10. John Markoff, "A Newer, Lonelier Crowd Emerges in Internet Study," *New York Times*, February 16, 2000, A1.

11. Elizabeth Weise, "Does the Internet Change News Reporting? Not Quite," *Media Studies Journal*, Spring 1997, 161.

12. Mitchell Stephens, *A History of News* (New York: Viking, 1988), 278.

13. Elmer W. Lower, "A Television Network Gathers the News,"

The Kennedy Assassination and the American Public, ed. Bradley S. Greenberg and Edwin B. Parker (Stanford: Stanford University Press, 1965), 72.

14. Reuven Frank, *Out of Thin Air* (New York: Simon & Schuster, 1991), 190.

15. Robert J. Donovan and Ray Scherer, *Unsilent Revolution* (New York: Cambridge University Press, 1992), 70.

16. Mary Ann Watson, *The Expanding Vista* (New York: Oxford University Press, 1990), 223.

17. Frank, *Out of Thin Air*, 190.

18. Watson, *The Expanding Vista*, 223.

19. Watson, *The Expanding Vista*, 216.

20. Ruth Leeds Love, "The Business of Television and the Black Weekend," in *The Kennedy Assassination and the American Public*, ed. Bradley S. Greenberg and Edwin B. Parker (Stanford: Stanford University Press, 1965), 83.

21. Donovan and Scherer, *Unsilent Revolution*, 70.

22. Andrew Ross Sorkin, "Diana's Death Expands Web's News Role," *New York Times*, September 8, 1997, C3.

23. Erik Barnouw, *The Image Empire* (New York: Oxford University Press, 1970), 3.

24. Arthur M. Schlesinger, *Robert Kennedy and His Times* (New York: Ballantine, 1979), 942.

25. Frank, *Out of Thin Air*, 262.

26. Michael Arlen, *Living-Room War* (New York: Penguin, 1982), 223.

27. Austin Ranney, *Channels of Power* (New York: Basic, 1983), 86.

28. Michael Kinsley, "Election Day Fraud on Television," *Time*, November 23, 1992, 84.

29. Roger Simon, *Show Time* (New York: Times Books, 1998), 251.

30. Simon, *Show Time*, 269.

31. Arlen, *Living-Room War*, 82–83.

32. Robert Lichter, "The Instant Replay War," in *The Media and the Gulf War*, ed. Hedrick Smith (Washington, D.C.: Seven Locks, 1992), 224.

33. Richard Valeriani, "Talking Back to the Tube," in *The Media and the Gulf War*, ed. Hedrick Smith (Washington, D.C.: Seven Locks, 1992), 232.

CHAPTER 2

1. "Wake Up and Smell the Ratings," report presented by Frank N. Magid Associates to the Radio and Television News Directors Association, September 1998, 9.

2. C. A. Tuggle and Suzanne Huffman, "Live News Reporting: Professional Judgment or Technological Pressure?" *Journal of Broadcasting and Electronic Media* 43, no. 4 (1999): 3.

3. Tuggle and Huffman, "Live News Reporting," 8.

4. Ted Koppel, "The Worst Is Yet to Come," *Washington Post*, April 3, 1994, G1.

5. James Sterngold, "After a Suicide: Questions on Lurid TV News," *New York Times*, May 2, 1998, A1.

6. Christian Berthelsen, "Soul-searching for TV in Los Angeles," *New York Times*, June 8, 1998, C6.

7. Patrick Rogers, "L.A.'s TV News: Pulling Away from Live Shots?" *American Journalism Review*, June 1998, 10.

8. Howard Rosenberg, "The Russian Roulette of Live News Coverage," *Los Angeles Times*, May 2, 1998, F1.

9. Walter Goodman, "On Covering a Suicide," *New York Times*, May 4, 1998, C5.

10. Sterngold, "After a Suicide," A1.

11. Berthelsen, "Soul-searching for TV," C6.

12. Lawrie Mifflin, "Big 3 Networks Forced to Revise News-Gathering Methods," *New York Times*, October 12, 1998, C1.

13. "Jonesboro: Were the Media Fair?" *Freedom Forum*, June 1998, 2.

14. "Jonesboro," 29.

15. Kelly Heyboer, "Web Feat," *American Journalism Review*, November 1998, 26.

16. Jacqueline Sharkey, "Starr Turn," *American Journalism Review*, November 1998, 22.

17. Heyboer, "Web Feat," 27.

18. Lou Cannon, *Official Negligence* (New York: Random House, 1997), 307.

19. Cannon, *Official Negligence*, 307.

20. Ron LaBrecque, "City of Anger," *Washington Journalism Review*, July-August 1992, 23.

21. LaBrecque, "City of Anger," 25.

22. Philip M. Taylor, *Global Communication, International Affairs, and the Media since 1945* (London: Routledge, 1997), 94.

23. Christopher Marquis, "Albright's Spokesman Ends Singular Tenure," *New York Times*, April 30, 2000, A10.

24. Lawrence Grossman, "A Television Plan for Covering the Next War," *Nieman Reports*, Summer 1991, 27.

25. Johanna Neuman, *Lights, Camera, War* (New York: St. Martin's, 1996), 215.

26. Michael Dobbs, "Foreign Policy by CNN," *Washington Post National Weekly Edition*, July 31, 1995, 24.

27. Steven Livingston, "The New Information Environment and Diplomacy" (paper prepared for the 1999 International Studies Association meeting, Washington, D.C., February 1999), 3.

CHAPTER 3

1. Susan J. Douglas, *Listening In* (New York: Times Books, 1999), 9.

2. Robert W. Decherd, "Localism: The Transformation into New Media" (speech to TVB Annual Marketing Conference, Las Vegas, April 2000), 1.

3. Pew Center, "Internet News Takes Off," 1.

4. Bill Carter, "Networks Take a Back Seat to Cable," *New York Times*, December 12, 1998, A14.

5. Decherd, "Localism," 2.

6. Lawrie Mifflin, "As Band of Channels Grows, Niche Programs Will Boom," *New York Times*, December 28, 1998, A1.

7. Jim Benning, "Inside the Online Newsroom: MSNBC.com," *Online Journalism Review*, October 27, 1998.

8. Alicia Shepard, "Webward Ho!" *American Journalism Review*, March 1997, 35.

9. Shepard, "Webward Ho!" 38.

10. Kari Huus, "Two Years of Living Electronically," *Nieman Reports*, Winter 1998, 63.

11. Huus, "Two Years," 63.

12. Huus, "Two Years," 64.

13. "Eighty Percent of Consumers Trust Online News as Much as Off-line," Jupiter Communications news release, November 19, 1998.

14. Steve Outing, "Local TV Affiliates Need Partners as They Awaken to the Web," *Editor and Publisher Interactive*, February 6, 1998, 2.

15. Lou Prato, "When TV Stations Venture Online," *American Journalism Review*, June 1998, 66.

16. Prato, "When TV Stations Venture Online," 66.

17. Anne Stuart, "Something Old, Something New," *CIO WebBusiness Magazine*, October 1, 1998, 6.

18. Prato, "When TV Stations Venture Online," 66.

19. <http://www.IBSYS.com> Accessed April 2000.

20. David Noack, "Extra! Extra! Read All about It! TV Web Site Acts Like Newspaper," *Editor and Publisher Interactive*, June 13, 1997, 2.

21. Noack, "Extra! Extra!" 2.

22. Noack, "Extra! Extra!" 2.

23. Dylan Loeb McClain, "Toronto TV Station Adopts Web-page Format," *New York Times*, December 27, 1999, C8.

24. "Eighty Percent of Consumers."

25. Pew Center, "The Internet News Audience Goes Ordinary," 68.

26. David Lieberman, "The Rise and Fall of 24-Hour Local News," *Columbia Journalism Review*, November-December, 1998, 55.

27. Steven Brill, "Must Merge TV," *Brill's Content*, February, 1999, 86.

28. Brill, "Must Merge TV," 86.

29. Pew Center, "The Internet News Audience Goes Ordinary," 14–15.

30. Pew Center, "The Internet News Audience Goes Ordinary," 15.

31. Pew Center, "The Internet News Audience Goes Ordinary," 16.

CHAPTER 4

1. "Caught in the Web," *Economist*, July 17, 1999, 18–19.

2. "Facts About Newspapers," Newspaper Association of America <http://www.naa.org/info/facts/18.html> Accessed May 2000.

3. Kevin Featherly, "Local Broadcasters: The Net's Sleeping Giant," *Online Journalism Review*, June 26, 1998, 2.

4. Rob Runett, "Defining 'Local' on the Web," *Digital Edge*, January 1999, 1.

5. Runett, "Defining 'Local,' " 2.

6. Rob Runett, "Knight Ridder New Media Officials Outline Approach to Content, Business Models," *Digital Edge*, December 1998, 5.

7. Runett, "Knight Ridder New Media Officials," 2.

8. Chip Brown, "Fear.com," *American Journalism Review*, June 1999, 55.

9. John Morton, "Protecting the Local Franchise On-line," *American Journalism Review*, April 1998, 60.

10. <http://www.realcities.com/aboutus/knightridder.htm> Accessed April 2000.

11. Geneva Overholser, "Newspapers Are Languishing as the Net Speeds Up," *Columbia Journalism Review*, March-April 2000, 60.

12. Richard Siklos, "If You Can't Beat 'Em . . ." *BusinessWeek*, January 18, 1999, 78.

13. "Caught in the Web," 17.

14. Katherine Yung, "Sponsoring the News On-line," *Dallas Morning News*, December 28, 1998, 1D.

15. Saul Hansell, "News-Ad Issues Arise in New Media," *New York Times*, December 8, 1997, C10.

16. Scott Kirsner, "Profits in Site?" *American Journalism Review*, December 1997, 42.

17. Kirsner, "Profits in Site?" 43.

18. Kirsner, "Profits in Site?" 42.

19. Rob Runett, "Research Estimate: Internet Newspapers Generate $203.7M in 1998," *Digital Edge*, January 1999, 1.

20. Kirsner, "Profits in Site?" 41.

21. Runett, "Research Estimate," 1.

22. Rob Runett, "The Cost of Doing Business On-line," *Digital Edge*, January 1999, 1.

23. Erin White, "Washington Post Stays the Course with Web Operations," *Wall Street Journal*, February 2, 2000, B4.

24. White, "Washington Post Stays the Course," B4.

25. Kirsner, "Profits in Site?" 43.

26. Runett, "The Cost of Doing Business On-line," 2.

27. Runett, "The Cost of Doing Business On-line," 4.

28. Howard Kurtz, "Free Slate," *Washington Post*, February 15, 1999, C4.

29. Felicity Barringer, "Web Surfers Want the News Fast and Free," *New York Times*, May 1, 2000, C12.

30. Kelly Heyboer, "Going Live," *American Journalism Review*, January-February 2000, 42.

31. J. D. Lasica, "Keeping On-line Staffers in Exile," *American Journalism Review*, May 1998, 72.

32. Philip Seib, ed., *Scandal or Substance: Covering the Character Issue in Campaign 2000* (Milwaukee: Marquette University, 2000), 80.

33. Jeffrey A. Perlman, "Lack of Job Standards Creates Confusion, Tension," *Online Journalism Review*, February 18, 1999, 3.

34. Matthew J. Rosenberg, "Web Publications Break Away from Print," *New York Times*, March 1, 1999, C13.

35. J. D. Lasica, "A Great Way to Strengthen Bonds," *American Journalism Review*, March 1998, 52.

36. Matt Welch, "The Corrector: Slipup.com," *Online Journalism Review*, March 4, 1999.

37. Frank Sennett, "Web Sites Aren't Forthcoming with Corrections," *Editor and Publisher Interactive*, February 8, 1999, 2–3.

38. Seib, *Scandal or Substance*, 83.

CHAPTER 5

1. "I-modest Success," *Economist*, March 11, 2000, 69.

2. Peter Burrows, "Beyond the PC," *BusinessWeek*, March 8, 1999, 84.

3. Burrows, "Beyond the PC," 86.

4. "Stretching Past Streaming," *Communicator*, April 2000, 14.

5. Lisa Napoli, "The Post-Lewinsky Winner Is the Web," *New York Times*, September 28, 1998, C7.

6. Pew Research Center for the People and the Press, "Online Polling Offers Mixed Results," news release, January 27, 1999, 1, 3.

7. Robert Schmidt, "New Media's Trial Run," *Brill's Content*, March 1999, 66.

8. Edwin Schlossberg, "A Question of Trust," *Brill's Content*, March 1999, 68.

9. Al Tompkins and Aly Colon, "Honeymoon Underway for Tam-

pa's Media Marriage" <http://www.poynter.org/centerpiece/042400.htm> Accessed May 2000.

10. Mike France, "Journalism's Online Credibility Gap," *Business-Week*, October 1999, 124.

11. Alicia Shepard, "Get Big or Get Out," *American Journalism Review*, March 2000, 27.

12. Shepard, "Get Big or Get Out," 29.

CHAPTER 6

1. Christopher Hanson, "The Dark Side of Online Scoops," *Columbia Journalism Review*, May-June 1997, 17.

2. Hanson, "The Dark Side of Online Scoops," 17.

3. Stacy Jones, "Free Press vs. Fair Trial," *Editor and Publisher*, March 5, 1997, 34.

4. Tom Kenworthy, "The McVeigh Story and Its Impact," *Washington Post*, March 2, 1997, A7.

5. J. D. Lasica, "Get It Fast, but Get It Right," *American Journalism Review*, October 1997, 64.

6. Howard Kurtz, "A Reporter's Net Loss," *Washington Post*, August 11, 1998, D1.

7. Larry J. Sabato, Mark Stencel, and S. Robert Lichter, *Peepshow* (Lanham, Md.: Rowman & Littlefield, 2000), 36.

8. David McClintick, "Town Crier for the New Age," *Brill's Content*, November 1998, 118.

9. Howard Kurtz, "Out There," *Washington Post*, March 28, 1999, F1.

10. Todd S. Purdum, "The Dangers of Dishing Dirt in Cyberspace," *New York Times*, August 17, 1997, E3.

11. Kurtz, "Out There," F1.

12. Matt Drudge, "Anyone with a Modem Can Report on the World" (speech to the National Press Club, Washington, D.C., June 2, 1998), 4.

13. Drudge, "Anyone with a Modem," 5.

14. Drudge, "Anyone with a Modem," 16, 10.

15. Drudge, "Anyone with a Modem," 18.

16. McClintick, "Town Crier for the New Age," 127.

17. Howard Kurtz, "Wall Street Journal Story Is Rushed onto the Web," *Washington Post*, February 5, 1998, A12.

18. Kurtz, "Wall Street Journal Story," A12.

19. Jack Shafer, "The Web Made Me Do It," *New York Times Magazine*, February 15, 1998, 24.

20. Tom Rosenstiel, "The Promise, and Perils, of Online Journalism," *Chronicle of Higher Education*, March 21, 1997, B6.

21. Bill Kovach, "Report from the Ombudsman," *Brill's Content*, February 1999, 23.

22. Runett, "Knight Ridder New Media," 1.

23. James M. Naughton, "This Just In! And This!" *New York Times*, February 1, 1998, WK17.

24. Barb Palser, "Charting New Terrain," *American Journalism Review*, November 1999, 27.

25. Amy Harmon, "Diana Photo Restarts Debate over Lack of Restrictions on Internet Postings," *New York Times*, September 22, 1997, C9.

26. J. D. Lasica, "Slow Down and Make Sure It's Right," *American Journalism Review*, April 1998, 56.

27. Dianne Lynch, "Without a Rulebook," *American Journalism Review*, January-February 1998, 40.

28. Linton Weeks, "Testing the Legal Limits of Cyberspace," *Washington Post National Weekly Edition*, September 8, 1997, 29.

29. Dean Rotbart, "An Intimate Look at Covering Littleton," *Columbia Journalism Review*, May-June 1999, 24.

30. Rotbart, "An Intimate Look at Covering Littleton," 24.

31. Bob Steele, "Guidelines for Covering Hostage-Taking Crises, Police Raids, Prison Uprisings, or Terrorist Actions," Radio and Television News Directors Foundation, 1999.

CHAPTER 7

1. Thomas L. Friedman, *The Lexus and the Olive Tree* (New York: Farrar, Straus & Giroux, 1999), 118.

2. Alex Kuczynski, "Time Warner to Shut Down Its Pathfinder Site on the Web," *New York Times*, April 27, 1999, C1.

3. Allison Fass, "Journalists among the Online Crowd," *New York Times*, March 20, 2000, C14.

4. Pew Research Center for the People and the Press, "Striking the Balance: Audience Interests, Business Pressures, and Journalists' Values," news release, March 30, 1999, V2.

5. Pew Research Center, "Striking the Balance," V3.

6. Pew Research Center, "Striking the Balance," V1.

7. Wendy Grossman, "Digital Diplomacy: A Two-edged Sword," *Daily Telegraph*, April 22, 1997, 9.

BIBLIOGRAPHY

BOOKS

Arlen, Michael. *Living-Room War*. New York: Penguin, 1982.

Barnouw, Erik. *The Image Empire*. New York: Oxford University Press, 1970.

——. *Tube of Plenty*. 2d ed. New York: Oxford University Press, 1990.

Cannon, Lou. *Official Negligence*. New York: Random House, 1997.

Dertouzos, Michael L. *What Will Be*. New York: HarperEdge/HarperCollins, 1997.

Diamond, Edwin, and Robert A. Silverman. *White House to Your House: Media and Politics in Virtual America*. Cambridge: MIT Press, 1995.

Donovan, Robert J., and Ray Scherer. *Unsilent Revolution*. New York: Cambridge University Press, 1992.

Douglas, Susan J. *Listening In*. New York: Times Books, 1999.

Frank, Reuven. *Out of Thin Air*. New York: Simon & Schuster, 1991.

Friedland, Lewis A. *Covering the World*. New York: Twentieth Century Fund, 1992.

Friedman, Thomas L. *The Lexus and the Olive Tree*. New York: Farrar, Straus & Giroux, 1999.

Greenberg, Bradley S., and Edwin B. Parker, eds. *The Kennedy Assassination and the American Public*. Stanford: Stanford University Press, 1965.

Grossman, Lawrence K. *The Electronic Republic*. New York: Viking, 1995.

Jamieson, Kathleen Hall, and David S. Birdsell. *Presidential Debates*. New York: Oxford University Press, 1988.

Minow, Newton N., John Bartlow Martin, and Lee M. Mitchell. *Presidential Television*. New York: Basic Books/Twentieth Century Fund, 1973.
Neuman, Johanna. *Lights, Camera, War*. New York: St. Martin's, 1996.
O'Neill, Michael J. *Terrorist Spectaculars: Should TV Coverage Be Curbed?* New York: Priority, 1986.
Parker, Richard. *Mixed Signals: The Prospects for Global Television News*. New York: Twentieth Century Fund, 1995.
Ranney, Austin. *Channels of Power*. New York: Basic, 1983.
Sabato, Larry J., Mark Stencel, and S. Robert Lichter. *Peepshow*. Lanham, Md.: Rowman & Littlefield, 2000.
Schlesinger, Arthur M. *Robert Kennedy and His Times*. New York: Ballantine, 1979.
Seib, Philip, ed. *Scandal or Substance: Covering the Character Issue in Campaign 2000*. Milwaukee: Marquette University, 2000.
Simon, Roger. *Show Time*. New York: Times Books, 1998.
Smith, Hedrick, ed. *The Media and the Gulf War*. Washington, D.C.: Seven Locks, 1992.
Stephens, Mitchell. *A History of News*. New York: Viking, 1988.
Strobel, Warren. *Late-Breaking Foreign Policy*. Washington, D.C.: U.S. Institute of Peace Press, 1997.
Taylor, Philip M. *Global Communications, International Affairs, and the Media since 1945*. London: Routledge, 1997.
Watson, Mary Ann. *The Expanding Vista*. New York: Oxford University Press, 1990.
Wiener, Robert. *Live from Baghdad*. New York: Doubleday, 1992.

ARTICLES AND REPORTS

Bark, Ed. "Viewers Tune In to Funeral." *Dallas Morning News*, September 9, 1997, 23A.
Barringer, Felicity. "Web Surfers Want the News Fast and Free." *New York Times*, May 1, 2000, C12.
Benning, Jim. "Inside the Online Newsroom: MSNBC.com." *Online Journalism Review*, October 27, 1998.
Berthelsen, Christian. "Soul-searching for TV in Los Angeles." *New York Times*, June 8, 1998, C6.

Brill, Steven. "Must Merge TV." *Brill's Content*, February 1999, 84–91.

Brodsky, Art. "The End of the Internet's Golden Age." *Washington Post National Weekly Edition*, September 15, 1997, 22.

Brown, Chip. "Fear.com." *American Journalism Review*, June 1999, 50–71.

Burrows, Peter. "Beyond the PC." *BusinessWeek*, March 8, 1999, 84–88.

———. "Cheap PCs." *BusinessWeek*, March 23, 1998, 28–32.

Carter, Bill. "Networks Take a Back Seat to Cable." *New York Times*, December 12, 1998, A14.

"Caught in the Web." *Economist*, July 17, 1999, 17–19.

Decherd, Robert W. "Localism: The Transformation into New Media." Speech to TVB Annual Marketing Conference, Las Vegas, April 11, 2000.

Dobbs, Michael. "Foreign Policy by CNN." *Washington Post National Weekly Edition*, July 31, 1995, 24.

Drudge, Matt. "Anyone with a Modem Can Report on the World." Speech to the National Press Club, Washington, D.C., June 2, 1998.

"Eighty Percent of Consumers Trust On-line News as Much as Off-line." Jupiter Communications news release, November 19, 1998.

Fass, Allison. "Journalists among the Online Crowd." *New York Times*, March 20, 2000, C14.

Featherly, Kevin. "Local Broadcasters: The Net's Sleeping Giant." *Online Journalism Review*, June 26, 1998.

France, Mike. "Journalism's Online Credibility Gap." *BusinessWeek*, October 11, 1999, 122–124.

Goldstein, Alan. "Use of Internet for Watching Video Hits All-Time High." *Dallas Morning News*, September 22, 1998, 7A.

Goodman, Walter. "On Covering a Suicide." *New York Times*, May 4, 1998, C5.

Grossman, Lawrence. "A Television Plan for the Next War." *Nieman Reports*, Summer 1991, 27–29.

Grossman, Wendy. "Digital Diplomacy a Two-Edged Sword." *Daily Telegraph*, April 22, 1997, 8.

Hall, Mark. "One-to-One Politics in Cyberspace." *Media Studies Journal*, Winter 1997, 97.

Hamm, Steve. "Would You Pay to Read *Slate*?" *BusinessWeek*, February 23, 1998, 120–122.

Hansell, Saul. "News-Ad Issues Arise in New Media." *New York Times*, December 8, 1997, C10.

Hanson, Christopher. "The Dark Side of Online Scoops." *Columbia Journalism Review*, May-June 1997, 17.

Harmon, Amy. "Diana Photo Restarts Debate over Lack of Restrictions on Internet Postings." *New York Times*, September 22, 1997, C9.

Harwood, Richard. "Hot Source for the Cyber-Age Media." *Washington Post*, October 20, 1997, A21.

Henneberger, Melinda. "Seeing Politics, and Mirrors, in the Coverage of Capitol Hill." *New York Times*, October 6, 1997, C1.

Heyboer, Kelly. "Going Live." *American Journalism Review*, January-February 2000, 39–43.

———. "Web Feat." *American Journalism Review*, November 1998, 26–28.

Huus, Kari. "Two Years of Living Electronically." *Nieman Reports*, Winter 1998, 63–64.

"I-modest Success." *Economist*, March 11, 2000, 69–70.

"Internet Radio." *Economist*, February 13, 1999, 10.

"Is It Tellynet or Netelly?" *Economist*, December 13, 1997, 10.

Jones, Stacy. "Free Press vs. Fair Trial." *Editor and Publisher*, March 5, 1997, 6–7.

"Jonesboro: Were the Media Fair?" *Freedom Forum*, June 1998.

Kenworthy, Tom. "The McVeigh Story and Its Impact." *Washington Post*, March 2, 1997, A7.

Kinsley, Michael. "Election Day Fraud on Television." *Time*, November 23, 1992, 84.

Kirsner, Scott. "The Breaking News Dilemma." *Columbia Journalism Review*, November-December 1997, 18.

———. "Profits in Site?" *American Journalism Review*, December 1997, 40.

Kohut, Andrew. "Internet Users Are on the Rise, but Public Affairs Interest Isn't." *Columbia Journalism Review*, January-February 2000, 68.

Koppel, Ted. "The Worst Is Yet to Come." *Washington Post*, April 3, 1994, G1.

Kovach, Bill. "Report from the Ombudsman." *Brill's Content*, February 1999, 23.

Kuczynski, Alex. "Time Warner to Shut Down Its Pathfinder Site on the Web." *New York Times*, April 27, 1999, C1.

Kurtz, Howard. "Cyber-Libel and the Web Gossip-Monger." *Washington Post*, August 15, 1997, G1.

———. "Free Slate." *Washington Post*, February 15, 1999, C4.

———. "N.Y. Times Online Ads: Custom Service." *Washington Post*, October 27, 1997, C1.

———. "Out There." *Washington Post*, March 28, 1999, F1.

———. "A Reporter's Net Loss." *Washington Post*, August 11, 1998, D1.

———. "Wall Street Journal Story Is Rushed onto the Web." *Washington Post*, February 5, 1998, A12.

LaBrecque, Ron. "City of Anger." *Washington Journalism Review*, July–August 1992, 20–28.

Lasica, J. D. "Get It Fast, but Get It Right." *American Journalism Review*, October 1997, 64.

———. "A Great Way to Strengthen Bonds." *American Journalism Review*, March 1998, 52.

———. "Keeping Online Staffers in Exile." *American Journalism Review*, May 1998, 72.

———. "Online News: A Credibility Gap Ahead?" *Online Journalism Review*, December 16, 1998.

———. "Online News Association Needs to Reach Out." *Online Journalism Review*, December 16, 1998.

———. "Slow Down and Make Sure It's Right." *American Journalism Review*, April 1998, 56.

———. "Video Comes to the World Wide Web." *American Journalism Review*, January–February 1998, 48.

Lichter, Robert. "The Instant Replay War." In *The Media and the Gulf War*. Edited by Hedrick Smith. Washington, D.C.: Seven Locks, 1992.

Lieberman, David. "The Rise and Rise of 24-Hour Local News." *Columbia Journalism Review*, November–December 1998, 54–57.

Livingston, Steven. "The New Information Environment and Diplomacy." Paper prepared for the 1999 International Studies Association meeting, Washington, D.C., February 16–20, 1999.

Love, Ruth Leeds. "The Business of Television and the Black Weekend." In *The Kennedy Assassination and the American Public*. Edited by Bradley S. Greenberg and Edwin B. Parker. Stanford: Stanford University Press, 1965, 73.

Lower, Elmer W. "A Television Network Gathers the News." In *The Kennedy Assassination and the American Public*, edited by Bradley S.

Greenberg and Edwin B. Parker, 67. Stanford: Stanford University Press, 1965.

Lule, Jack. "The Power and Pitfalls of Journalism in the Hypertext Era." *Chronicle of Higher Education*, August 7, 1998, B7.

Lynch, Dianne. "Without a Rulebook." *American Journalism Review*, January-February 1998, 40.

Markoff, John. "A Newer, Lonelier Crowd Emerges in Internet Study." *New York Times*, February 16, 2000, A1.

Marquis, Christopher. "Albright's Spokesman Ends Singular Tenure." *New York Times*, April 30, 2000, A10.

McClain, Dylan Loeb. "Toronto TV Station Adopts Web-Page Format." *New York Times*, December 27, 1999, C8.

McClintick, David. "Town Crier for the New Age." *Brill's Content*, November 1998, 113–127.

Mifflin, Lawrie. "As Band of Channels Grows, Niche Programs Will Boom." *New York Times*, December 28, 1998, A1.

———. "Big 3 Networks Forced to Revise News-Gathering Methods." *New York Times*, October 12, 1998, C1.

———. "Watch the Tube or Watch the Computer?" *New York Times*, February 1, 1999, C8.

Moisy, Claude. "Myths of the Global Information Village." *Foreign Policy* 107 (Summer 1997): 78.

Morton, John. "Protecting the Local Franchise Online." *American Journalism Review*, April 1998, 60.

Napoli, Lisa. "The Post-Lewinsky Winner Is the Web." *New York Times*, September 28, 1998, C7.

Naughton, James M. "This Just In! And This!" *New York Times*, February 1, 1998, WK17.

"New Media Hurt TV News, Not Newspapers." *Freedom Forum News* 4, no. 10 (1997): 5.

Noack, David. "Extra! Extra! Read All about It! TV Web Site Acts Like Newspaper." *Editor and Publisher Interactive*, June 13, 1997.

"Online Press Struggles for Equal Credentials." *Freedom Forum and Newseum News*, September 1997, 7.

Outing, Steve. "Local TV Affiliates Need Partners as They Awaken to the Web." *Editor and Publisher Interactive*, February 6, 1998.

Overholser, Geneva. "Newspapers Are Languishing as the Net Speeds Up." *Columbia Journalism Review*, March-April 2000, 60–61.

Palser, Barb. "Charting New Terrain." *American Journalism Review*, November 1999, 25–31.

Pavlik, John V. "The Future of On-Line Journalism." *Columbia Journalism Review*, July-August 1997, 30–36.

"PC Industry Grew 15 Percent in 1998." Associated Press wire, January 29, 1999.

Perlman, Jeffrey A. "Lack of Job Standards Creates Confusion, Tension." *Online Journalism Review*, February 18, 1999.

Pew Research Center for the People and the Press. "The Internet News Audience Goes Ordinary." News release, January 14, 1999.

———. "Internet News Takes Off." News release, June 8, 1998.

———. "Online Polling Offers Mixed Results." News release, January 27, 1999.

———. "Stock Market Down, New Media Up." News release, November 9, 1997.

———. "Striking the Balance: Audience Interests, Business Pressures, and Journalists' Values." News release, March 30, 1999.

Pope, Kyle. "For the Media, Diana's Funeral Prompts Debate." *Wall Street Journal*, September 8, 1997, B1.

"Portals Emerge as Dominant Source for Online News." Jupiter Communications news release, December 8, 1998.

Prato, Lou. "L.A.: The TV News Trendsetter." *American Journalism Review*, January-February 1998, 46.

———. "When TV Stations Venture Online." *American Journalism Review*, June 1998, 66.

Purdum, Todd S. "The Dangers of Dishing Dirt in Cyberspace." *New York Times*, August 17, 1997, E3.

Regan, Tom. "On the Web, Speed Instead of Accuracy." *Nieman Reports*, Spring 1998, 81.

Rogers, Patrick. "L.A.'s TV News: Pulling Away from Live Shots?" *American Journalism Review*, June 1998, 10.

Rosenberg, Howard. "The Russian Roulette of Live News Coverage." *Los Angeles Times*, May 2, 1998, F1.

Rosenberg, Matthew J. "Web Publications Break Away from Print." *New York Times*, March 1, 1999, C13.

Rosenstiel, Tom. "The Promise, and Perils, of On-Line Journalism." *Chronicle of Higher Education*, March 21, 1997, B6.

Rotbart, Dean. "An Intimate Look at Covering Littleton." *Columbia Journalism Review*, May-June 1999, 24–25.

Runett, Rob. "The Cost of Doing Business Online." *Digital Edge*, January 1999.

———. "Defining 'Local' On the Web." *Digital Edge*, January 1999.

———. "Knight Ridder New Media Officials Outline Approach to Content, Business Models." *Digital Edge*, December 1998.

———. "Research Estimate: Internet Newspapers Generate $203.7M in 1998." *Digital Edge*, January 1999.

Rutenberg, Jim. "Watching Elian Gonzalez." *New York Times*, April 26, 2000, B7.

Schlossberg, Edwin. "A Question of Trust." *Brill's Content*, March 1999, 68–70.

Schmidt, Robert. "New Media's Trial Run." *Brill's Content*, March 1999, 66.

Scott, Janny. "Internet Story Revives Questions on Standards." *New York Times*, February 6, 1998, A12.

———. "Rules in Flux: News Organizations Face Tough Calls on Unverified 'Facts.' " *New York Times*, January 27, 1998, A13.

Segal, David. "Modem Times, Ancient Ways." *Washington Post*, August 9, 1997, A1.

Sennett, Frank. "Web Sites Aren't Forthcoming with Corrections." *Editor & Publisher Interactive*, February 8, 1999.

Shafer, Jack. " 'The Web Made Me Do It.' " *New York Times Magazine*, February 15, 1998, 24–25.

Sharkey, Jacqueline. "Starr Turn." *American Journalism Review*, November 1998, 20–25.

Shepard, Alicia. "Get Big or Get Out." *American Journalism Review*, March 2000, 22–29.

———. "Webward Ho!" *American Journalism Review*, March 1997, 32–38.

Siklos, Richard. "If You Can't Beat 'Em . . ." *BusinessWeek*, January 18, 1999, 78–80.

Smith, Gordon S. "Driving Diplomacy into Cyberspace." *World Today*, June 1997, 156.

Sorkin, Andrew Ross. "Diana's Death Expands Web's News Role." *New York Times*, September 8, 1997, C3.

Steele, Bob. "Guidelines for Covering Hostage-Taking Crises, Police Raids, Prison Uprisings, or Terrorist Actions." Radio and Television News Directors Foundation, April 1999.

Sterngold, James. "After a Suicide, Questions on Lurid TV News." *New York Times*, May 2, 1998, A1.

Streitfeld, David, and Michael Colton. "A Web of Lies." *Washington Post*, August 9, 1997, B1.

"Stretching Past Streaming." *Communicator*, April 2000, 14.

Stuart, Anne. "Something Old, Something New." *WebBusiness Magazine*, October 1, 1998.

Tompkins, Al, and Aly Colon. "Honeymoon Underway for Tampa's Media Marriage." <http://www.poynter.org-centerpiece-042400.htm> Accessed May 2000.

Tuggle, C. A., and Suzanne Huffman. "Live News Reporting: Professional Judgment or Technological Pressure?" *Journal of Broadcasting and Electronic Media* 434 (1999): 492–505.

Valeriani, Richard. "Talking Back to the Tube." In *The Media and the Gulf War*. Edited by Hedrick Smith. Washington, D.C.: Seven Locks, 1992.

"Wake Up and Smell the Ratings." Report presented by Frank N. Magid Associates to the Radio and Television News Directors Association, September 1998.

Weeks, Linton. "Testing the Legal Limits of Cyberspace." *Washington Post National Weekly Edition*, September 8, 1997, 29.

Weise, Elizabeth. "Does the Internet Change News Reporting? Not Quite." *Media Studies Journal*, Spring 1997, 159.

Welch, Matt. "The Corrector: Slipup.com." *Online Journalism Review*, March 4, 1999.

White, Erin. "Washington Post Stays the Course with Web Operations." *Wall Street Journal*, February 2, 2000, B4.

Yung, Katherine. "Sponsoring the News Online." *Dallas Morning News*, December 28, 1998, 1D.

Zimmermann, Tim. "All Propaganda, All the Time." *U.S. News and World Report*, November 11, 1996, 48.

USEFUL WEB SITES

These Web sites have information about the changing news business, often with links to additional sites.

American Society of Newspaper
Editors   *www.asne.org*

Editor and Publisher Online   *www.mediainfo.com*
Freedom Forum   *www.freedomforum.org*
Internet Advertising Bureau   *www.iab.net*
InterSurvey   *www.intersurvey.com*
Media Metrix   *www.mediametrix.com*
National Association of
  Broadcasters   *www.nab.org*
Newspaper Association of
  America   *www.naa.org*
Nielsen/NetRatings   *www.nielsennetratings.com*
Online Journalism Review   *ojr.usc.edu*
Online News Association   *www.onlinenewsassociation.org*
Pew Research Center for the
  People and the Press   *www.peoplepress.org*
Poynter Institute   *poynter.org*
Radio-Television News Directors
  Association   *www.rtnda.org*
Society of Professional Journalists *www.spj.org*

INDEX

ABOUT THE AUTHOR

Philip Seib is the Lucius W. Nieman Professor of Journalism at Marquette University. He is the author of eleven books, including *Headline Diplomacy: How News Coverage Affects Foreign Policy* and *Campaigns and Conscience: The Ethics of Political Journalism.* He is also a veteran television and newspaper journalist, covering politics and social issues.